CAMBRIDGE NATIONAL LEVEL 1/LEVEL 2

Child Development

Student Book

Brenda Baker, Louise Burnham &
Katherine Stapleton

CAMBRIDGE
UNIVERSITY PRESS

University Printing House, Cambridge CB2 8BS, United Kingdom

One Liberty Plaza, 20th Floor, New York, NY 10006, USA

477 Williamstown Road, Port Melbourne, VIC 3207, Australia

314–321, 3rd Floor, Plot 3, Splendor Forum, Jasola District Centre, New Delhi – 110025, India

103 Penang Road, #05–06/07, Visioncrest Commercial, Singapore 238467

Cambridge University Press is part of the University of Cambridge.

It furthers the University's mission by disseminating knowledge in the pursuit of education, learning and research at the highest international levels of excellence.

www.cambridge.org
Information on this title: www.cambridge.org/9781009127905

First published 2022

20 19 18 17 16 15 14 13 12 11 10 9 8 7 6 5 4 3 2 1

Printed in Italy by LEGO

A catalogue record for this publication is available from the British Library

ISBN 978-1-00912790-5 Paperback with Digital Access (2 Years)
ISBN 978-1-00912571-0 Digital Student Book (2 Years)
ISBN 978-1-00912572-7 1 Year site license

Additional resources for this publication at www.cambridge.org/9781009127905

The teaching content of this resource is endorsed by OCR for use with specification Level 1/ Level 2 Cambridge Nationals in Child Development at a glance (J809).

All references to assessment, including assessment preparation and practice questions of any format/style are the publisher's interpretation of the specification and are not endorsed by OCR.

This resource was designed for use with the version of the specification available at the time of publication. However, as specifications are updated over time, there may be contradictions between the resource and the specification, therefore please use the information on the latest specification and Sample Assessment Materials at all times when ensuring students are fully prepared for their assessments.

Endorsement indicates that a resource is suitable to support delivery of an OCR specification, but it does not mean that the endorsed resource is the only suitable resource to support delivery, or that it is required or necessary to achieve the qualification.

OCR recommends that teachers consider using a range of teaching and learning resources based on their own professional judgement for their students' needs. OCR has not paid for the production of this resource, nor does OCR receive any royalties from its sale. For more information about the endorsement process, please visit the OCR website.

....

....

Contents

Acknowledgements

The authors and publishers acknowledge the following sources of copyright material and are grateful for the permissions granted. While every effort has been made, it has not always been possible to identify the sources of all the material used, or to trace all copyright holders. If any omissions are brought to our notice, we will be happy to include the appropriate acknowledgements on reprinting.

R057 TA3 Boys 0–1 year centile chart reproduced with kind permission of the RCPCH and Harlow Printing Limited; **R057 TA4** The BSI Kitemark logo is used with permission from the British Standards Institution; **R057 TA4** The Lion Mark is used with permission from the British Toy and Hobby Association (BTHA)

Thanks to the following for permission to reproduce images:

Cover Peter Dazeley/GI; *Inside* **R057:** Nikola Stojadinovic/GI; Ariel Skelley/GI; Luis Alvarez/GI; Fertnig/GI; Ed Reschke/GI; Peter Dazeley/GI; Artinun Prekmoung/GI; BSIP/GI; Xavierarnau/GI; AlonzoDesign/GI; Marochkina/GI; AlonzoDesign/GI; Paul Richardson/GI; Paul Richardson/GI; Caroline Purser/GI; Ugurhan/GI; ViewStock/GI; Monkeybusinessimages/GI; Jon Feingersh Photography Inc/GI; Monkeybusinessimages/GI; Prostock-Studio/GI; Aldona/GI; Aldona/GI; Ippei Naoi/GI; Senkumar Alfred/GI; FatCamera/GI; ER Productions Limited/GI; Dimitri Otis/GI; Roy JAMES Shakespeare/GI; isayildiz/GI; SolStock/GI; Ariel Skelley/GI; design/GI; Rob Lewine/GI; Monkeybusinessimages/GI; Roberto Westbrook/GI; Jose Luis Pelaez Inc/GI; Halfpoint/GI; Image Source/GI; jure/GI; Bgton/GI; PansLaos/GI; Green Cross Code icon © 2015 North Yorkshire County Council; FG Trade/GI; **R058:** Jamie Grill/GI; Lostinbids/GI; Rawpixel/GI; Adam Gault/GI; Perkmeup/GI; Flubydust/GI; Mrs/GI; Anna Pekunova/GI; Sturti/GI; Oksana Shufrych/GI; Luplupme/GI; JohnAlexandr/GI; Andrea Kennard Photography/GI; Joni_R/GI; Mrs/GI; M-Image/GI; Kate_sept2004/GI; Chaluk/GI; The Eatwell Guide, Crown Copyright; New 5532 guide to portion size for preschoolers Reproduced with the permission of British Nutrition Foundation; Athima Tongloom/GI; OJO Images/GI; Design/GI; Jamie Grill/GI; Onebluelight/GI; M-Image/GI; Roberto Westbrook/GI; Sod Tatong/GI; Floortje/GI; Kathrin Ziegler/GI; Ferrantraite/GI; JGI/Jamie Grill/GI; **R059:** FatCamera/GI; FatCamera/GI; MachineHeadz/GI; Minchen Liang/GI; Jose Luis Pelaez Inc/GI; Alexandra Jursova/GI; Alvarez/GI; Park Lane Pictures/GI; Medioimages/Photodisc/GI; Michael H/GI; FatCamera/GI; Fly View Productions/GI; Fig. 3.8 Brenda Baker; Aldomurillo/GI; Cavan Images/GI; Lostinbids/GI; Dmphoto/GI; Ariel Skelley/GI; Alfredo Lietor/GI; Valeryprint2d/GI; StefaNikolic/GI; ChrisGorgio/GI; Liam Norris/GI; Goldfaery/GI; SDI Productions/GI; Westend61/GI; PeopleImages/GI; RainStar/GI; Sturti/GI; Maskot/GI; Westend61/GI; FatCamera/GI; Westend61/GI

Key: GI = Getty Images

The authors would like to thank Eleanor Barber, Jilly Hunt and Sarah Porter for all their help and support during this project. They would also like to thank the many individuals, health and early years settings that have over the years provided them with inspiration. Brenda Baker would also like to thank Lio, Luc, Ava and Isabel for kindly providing drawings and writing to demonstrate writing development. Louise Burnham would like to dedicate her work on this book to Tom, Lizi and Freddie.

About your Cambridge National course and qualification

Working in the childcare sector can be very rewarding. The Cambridge National Child Development course will help you to develop knowledge, understanding and practical skills that can be used in real-life situations within the sector.

You will learn about what a child needs to thrive from pre-conception, through birth to five years old. You will build confidence and independence in practical skills, such as preparing a feed or meal for a child. You will become alert to potential hazards in a child's environment, both at home and in a childcare setting. You will learn about development norms and how to support a young child to progress by planning suitable play activities.

During your Child Development course, you will also develop learning and skills that can be used in other life or work situations, such as skills in research and communication. Your Cambridge National in Child Development can help you progress on to other related study, such as further qualifications in Childcare, Health and Social Care, Psychology, Sociology and Biology.

How you will be assessed

You have to complete three mandatory units.

Mandatory units

- R057: Health and well-being for child development. You will take a written exam for this unit. The exam lasts for 1 hour 15 minutes, and is worth 70 marks. The exam is set and marked by OCR.

- R058: Create a safe environment and understand the nutritional needs of children from birth to five years. You will be given a set assignment with four practical tasks, which is worth 60 marks.

- R059: Understand the development of a child from one to five years. You will be given a set assignment with two practical tasks, which is worth 60 marks.

How to use this book

Throughout this book, you will notice lots of different features that will help your learning. These are explained below.

These features at the start of each unit give you guidance on the Topic Area, what you will learn and how you will be assessed.

Thought-provoking questions at the start of units and topics will get you thinking about the subject.

This section gives you information about what content is covered in the topic.

Case studies based on real-life situations put key concepts and practices into context. The accompanying questions check your understanding and challenge you to take your learning further.

R057   Health and well-being for child development

What will you learn in this unit?

In any role as a childcare or health professional you will need to understand the care and development needs of children of all ages, including the pre-conception stage, in order to help you to care for and support children and their parents. It is important to understand pre-conception health and the factors that affect a woman becoming pregnant and staying healthy throughout her pregnancy. In this unit you will learn about the importance of pre-conception health as well as birth and postnatal care, and the prevention and management of childhood illnesses.

In this unit you will learn about:

- pre-conception health and reproduction **TA1**
- antenatal care and preparation for birth **TA2**
- postnatal checks, postnatal care and the conditions for development **TA3**
- childhood illnesses and a child-safe environment **TA4**.

How you will be assessed

This unit will be externally assessed by a 1-hour 15-minute written exam that is worth 40% of your overall mark for this qualification. In the exam, you will be expected to show that you understand this unit by answering questions that require you to analyse and evaluate your understanding in relation to health and well-being for child development.

Pre-conception health and reproduction   TA1

TA1

Pre-conception health and reproduction

Let's get started   1

Why do parents need to think about their health before trying to have a baby? Do both parents need to do this?

Figure 1.1: What factors affect pre-conception?

What will you learn?

- Factors affecting **pre-conception** health for women and men.
- Other factors affecting pre-conception health for women.
- Types of **contraception** methods and their advantages and disadvantages.
- The structure and function of the reproductive systems.
- How **reproduction** takes place.
- The signs and symptoms of pregnancy.

11

Case study

Marietta and Geoff

Marietta and her husband Geoff have two children and are considering using natural methods of family planning. Marietta is on long-term medication which would reduce the effectiveness of most hormonal methods. They have used barrier methods in the past but find them intrusive. They do not want to have any more children. They have sex regularly.

Figure 1.8: Marietta and Geoff with their children

Check your understanding

1. Why do you think natural methods are a good form of contraception for Marietta and Geoff?
2. Describe the advantages and disadvantages of natural methods of contraception.
3. Evaluate whether these methods are the best choice for Marietta and Geoff.

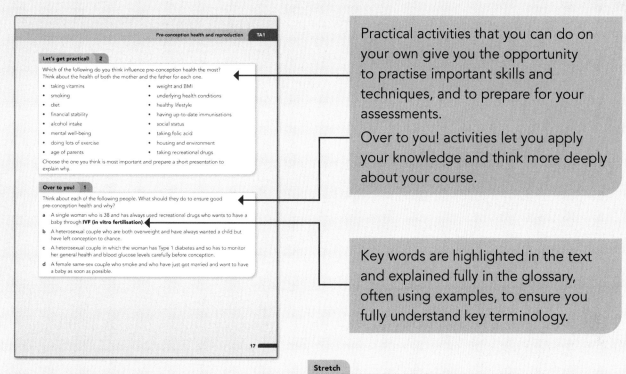

Practical activities that you can do on your own give you the opportunity to practise important skills and techniques, and to prepare for your assessments.

Over to you! activities let you apply your knowledge and think more deeply about your course.

Key words are highlighted in the text and explained fully in the glossary, often using examples, to ensure you fully understand key terminology.

Stretch

Lucy is four years old and will start school next month. She lives with her parents and her baby brother Zac in a small basement flat with a garden. There have been some signs of damp in the flat which is a concern with a new baby.

The family are close and regularly see both sets of grandparents but have very little money as Lucy's father has been made redundant from his job and her mother is still on maternity leave after having her baby brother. The landlord has threatened to evict them if they are unable to pay the rent for a third month running, although her maternal grandmother has said that they can stay with her if they need to. The family have been getting very little sleep as the baby does not yet sleep through the night.

Stretch activities and questions give you the opportunity to try more challenging questions and to extend your knowledge.

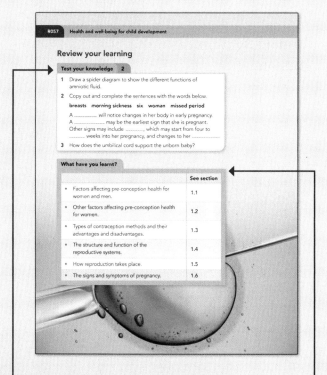

These question boxes give you regular opportunities to test your knowledge so that you feel ready for your exam or assessment.

Summary sections help you review your learning, to check you understand key concepts and can apply your learning. They also show you where to look back for more information if you need to read it again.

Support for you

Our resources in this series are designed to work together to help you with your Cambridge National course.

Your Student Book is where you will find the core information you need. This will help you with your knowledge and understanding of the subject. Information is arranged by Unit and then by Topic Area, so you can easily find what you're looking for. Questions and activities will help you to apply your knowledge and understanding and to develop practical skills. You can assess your progress with the Test Your Knowledge questions. When you've completed the quiz, check your answers in the digital edition.

Your Revision Guide and Workbook supports you with the externally assessed unit of your course. The exam preparation section offers advice to help you get ready for this assessment. The revision guide section provides concise outlines of the core knowledge you need. Each page focuses on a small piece of learning to help you break your revision up into manageable chunks. The workbook section brings your revision and learning together with practice questions. Digital quizzes help you to understand the language used in your assessment and to check your knowledge and understanding of key concepts.

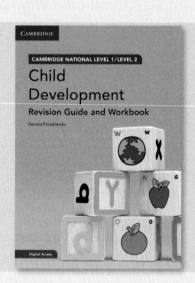

The Teacher's Resource is a rich bank of ideas to help your teacher create engaging lessons to meet the needs of your class. It contains PowerPoint slides, worksheets and audio-visual material, in addition to activity and delivery ideas that can be personalised for your lessons. Digital quizzes help test your understanding and unlock the language used in assessment.

R057 Health and well-being for child development

Let's get started

What kinds of health factors can parents consider when trying to have a baby?

When should they think about them?

What will you learn in this unit?

In any role as a childcare or health professional you will need to understand the care and development needs of children of all ages, including the pre-conception stage, in order to help you to care for and support children and their parents. It is important to understand pre-conception health and the factors that affect a woman becoming pregnant and staying healthy throughout her pregnancy. In this unit you will learn about the importance of pre-conception health as well as birth and postnatal care, and the prevention and management of childhood illnesses.

In this unit you will learn about:

- pre-conception health and reproduction **TA1**

- antenatal care and preparation for birth **TA2**

- postnatal checks, postnatal care and the conditions for development **TA3**

- childhood illnesses and a child-safe environment **TA4**.

How you will be assessed

This unit will be externally assessed by a 1-hour 15-minute written exam that is worth 40% of your overall mark for this qualification. In the exam, you will be expected to show that you understand this unit by answering questions that require you to analyse and evaluate your understanding in relation to health and well-being for child development.

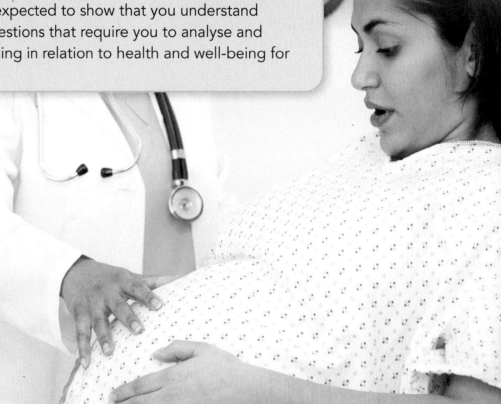

Pre-conception health and reproduction

Let's get started   1

Why do parents need to think about their health before trying to have a baby? Do both parents need to do this?

Figure 1.1: What factors affect pre-conception?

What will you learn?

- Factors affecting **pre-conception** health for women and men.

- Other factors affecting pre-conception health for women.

- Types of **contraception** methods and their advantages and disadvantages.

- The structure and function of the reproductive systems.

- How **reproduction** takes place.

- The signs and symptoms of pregnancy.

1.1 Factors affecting pre-conception health for women and men

When we think about health and well-being for child development, it is important to go right back to the start – to the pre-conception stage. We need to help parents to understand their **pre-conception health** and to consider things such as their **lifestyle choices**. This will help them to ensure healthy and positive outcomes for their baby.

Pre-conception health means the physical health of both partners who are planning to have a baby. Although it is natural to think that the health of the mother is important, the health of the father will also have an influence on a healthy conception. It is a good idea for both parents to start planning for a healthy baby even before starting to conceive. Pre-conception health is an area which parents may feel they have some control over when planning a baby. Making proactive choices before conception means that the baby has the best possible chance of growing and developing healthily.

A range of factors affect pre-conception health and the chance that men and women have of conceiving (see Figure 1.2).

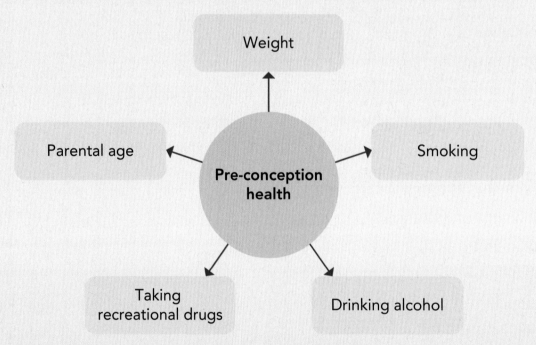

Figure 1.2: The factors which impact on pre-conception health for men and women

Weight

Both parents should be a healthy weight. Being overweight or **obese** affects both men's and women's **fertility**. A high **body mass index (BMI)** (more than 30) can mean that a woman's chance of getting pregnant is lower. Obesity can affect fertility in a man by reducing the amount and quality of his sperm.

Smoking

Smoking can have a dramatic effect on men's and women's fertility. Research from a charity that helps babies has shown that women who smoke are twice as likely to have fertility problems than those who do not. It is likely that getting pregnant will take longer as smoking affects the lining of the uterus. The risk of fertility problems increases with the number of cigarettes a woman smokes each day.

Passive smoking – breathing in smoke from someone else's cigarette – can also affect a woman's fertility. In men, smoking can affect sperm count as well as causing **impotence** (a medical condition when a man can't have or can't maintain an erection and so can't have sex).

Drinking alcohol

Alcohol can affect fertility for men and women in a number of ways. For women, heavy drinking in particular can cause problems with **menstruation** (periods). This means that they are less likely to **ovulate**. It is recommended that women trying to conceive should not drink at all. For men, alcohol can affect the quality of their sperm as well as potentially lowering **testosterone** and causing impotence.

Taking recreational drugs

Taking recreational drugs (for example cannabis, ecstasy or amphetamines) can cause fertility problems in both men and women, as well as affect general well-being. In women, taking drugs may cause their **hormones** to become imbalanced. In men, drugs may affect their sperm quality and lower their levels of testosterone.

Parental age

The fertility of both men and women is affected as they age, mainly due to a decline in the quality of eggs and sperm.

For women, age is the most important factor when trying to get pregnant. Both the number and quality of a woman's eggs reduces in her late 20s and early 30s, and in particular after the age of 35. This affects her ability to get pregnant and increases the risk of miscarriage. By the age of 45, it is much more difficult for a woman to conceive naturally.

In men, fertility also decreases with age, although this does not follow such a predictable pattern. Sperm quality gradually decreases over time, although it is possible for much older men to become fathers.

Let's get practical! **1**

Design a quiz for potential parents about some of the factors which affect pre-conception health.
For example:

Do you smoke?	Yes / No

If yes, you should consider stopping because …

1.2 Other factors affecting pre-conception health for women

Some aspects of pre-conception health are more important for women. This is because after conception the baby will be living and growing inside the mother's body and will take in nutrients through the **placenta** (see Section 1.5).

Folic acid

Folic acid (sometimes called vitamin folate or vitamin B9) is part of the group of B vitamins, which help the body to make healthy red blood cells. One of the reasons that it should be taken more than other supplements is that our bodies are not able to store it very well.

NHS guidelines recommend that women who are planning to get pregnant should take folic acid every day for 2 to 3 months before conception and for the first 12 weeks of pregnancy. This is because although vitamin B9 is found in certain foods such as green vegetables and citrus fruits, it is difficult to get the recommended amount for a healthy pregnancy through food alone (see Figure 1.3).

As well as being responsible for making healthy blood cells, folic acid is linked to the formation of the **neural tube** in babies. The neural tube is the early development of the baby's central nervous system – the brain, skull and spinal cord. This is formed in the embryo very soon after conception (that is, about four to six weeks after the first day of a woman's last menstrual period) – so sometimes before the mother knows that she is pregnant. (See Figure 1.4.) If there is not enough folate in her system, the baby is more likely to have a birth defect such as open spina bifida or anencephaly. (For information about screening for these conditions, see Section 2.2.)

In some cases, a woman may be at more risk of being affected in pregnancy by neural tube defects. This may be:

- if she has diabetes or epilepsy
- if she or the father have a family history of neural tube defects in a previous pregnancy
- if she drinks alcohol heavily.

In these cases, the woman will benefit from a higher than normal dose of folic acid before trying to become pregnant.

Figure 1.3: As well as taking folic acid, women who want to get pregnant are advised to eat more food containing folate. Can you name these foods?

Figure 1.4: The neural tube develops in the embryo early on in pregnancy.

Up-to-date immunisations

it is important that a woman's **immunisations** are up to date before conception. This is because the health of both mother and baby may be affected if the mother's immunisations are not up to date and she is unwell during or after pregnancy. It is not safe to give all **vaccines** during pregnancy. See Table 1.1 for more information.

Table 1.1: Vaccines and pregnancy

Name of vaccine	Reason for use	Can be given during pregnancy?
Rubella (German measles)	The rubella virus is very serious if caught during pregnancy. It can cause congenital rubella syndrome (CRS), which can lead to a range of health conditions in the baby, including deafness, blindness, heart problems or even death. Women should have had two doses of the rubella vaccine before becoming pregnant.	No
MMR (measles, mumps and rubella)	If women have not had the rubella vaccine or the infection itself, the MMR vaccine (which contains protection against rubella) can be given up to a month before pregnancy.	Not recommended
Whooping cough (pertussis)	Whooping cough is highly infectious and affects a person's ability to breathe when coughing. Whooping cough *can be* very dangerous in young babies and lead to pneumonia and brain damage. Having the injection during pregnancy will pass on some of the antibodies through the placenta and give the unborn baby some protection.	Yes, between the 16th and 32nd weeks
Flu	The flu vaccine can be given safely at any time during pregnancy. It should be given to pregnant women as early as possible in the flu season (October to March). As pregnant women have a weakened immune system they may be more likely to have complications such as pneumonia if they catch flu. Flu in the mother can be serious for unborn and newborn babies – it can lead to **stillbirth** and death. Having the injection during pregnancy will pass on some of the antibodies through the placenta and give the unborn baby some protection.	Yes
COVID-19	COVID-19 can be dangerous at all ages. It is safe for those who are trying for a baby, those who are pregnant and those who are breastfeeding to have the COVID-19 immunisations.	Yes

Let's get practical!   2

Which of the following do you think influence pre-conception health the most?
Think about the health of both the mother and the father for each one.

- taking vitamins
- smoking
- diet
- financial stability
- alcohol intake
- mental well-being
- doing lots of exercise
- age of parents
- weight and BMI
- underlying health conditions
- healthy lifestyle
- having up-to-date immunisations
- social status
- taking folic acid
- housing and environment
- taking recreational drugs

Choose the one you think is most important and prepare a short presentation to explain why.

Over to you!   1

Think about each of the following people. What should they do to ensure good pre-conception health and why?

a   A single woman who is 38 and has always used recreational drugs who wants to have a baby through **IVF (in vitro fertilisation)**.

b   A heterosexual couple who are both overweight and have always wanted a child but have left conception to chance.

c   A heterosexual couple in which the woman has Type 1 diabetes and so has to monitor her general health and blood glucose levels carefully before conception.

d   A female same-sex couple who smoke and who have just got married and want to have a baby as soon as possible.

1.3 Types of contraception methods and their advantages and disadvantages

Let's get started   2

Think about what you know about different types of contraception. Why do you think it is it important for partners to know about and understand the different types before making a choice?

Barrier methods

Barrier methods prevent the male sperm from reaching the female egg. They are known as barrier methods as some form of a barrier to **fertilisation** is used. There are several different types of barrier methods, some of which are used by men and others by women.

Male condoms

A male condom or sheath is put on the erect penis during intercourse (sex). It prevents pregnancy by stopping the sperm from meeting the egg. Male condoms are widely available at pharmacies. They are available without prescription or GP appointment (see Figure 1.5).

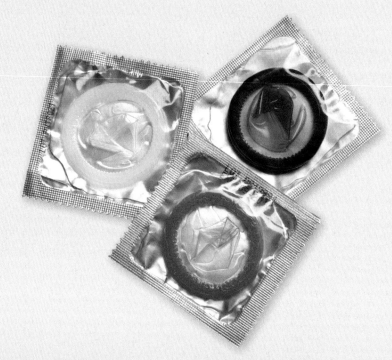

Female condoms

A female condom is placed inside the vagina before intercourse. It prevents pregnancy by stopping sperm from reaching the uterus. Female condoms are also available from pharmacies without a prescription.

Figure 1.5: How is this contraception method used to prevent pregnancy?

Diaphragm or cap

A diaphragm or cap is placed over the cervix (the entrance to the uterus) before intercourse along with spermicide (a cream that kills sperm). It prevents pregnancy by stopping sperm from reaching the uterus. Diaphragms are available free through GPs and family planning clinics and need some instruction and practice for correct use. See Table 1.2 for more information.

Table 1.2: The advantages, disadvantages and effectiveness of barrier methods of contraception

Type of barrier method	Advantages	Disadvantages	Effectiveness when used correctly (Source: NHS)
Male condom	Easily available. No preparation needed. Helps to protect against sexually transmitted diseases (STIs). No side effects. Relatively cheap.	If used incorrectly or torn, likely to be ineffective.	98%
Female condom	Available without prescription or GP appointment. No preparation needed. Helps to protects against STIs. No side effects.	If used incorrectly or torn, likely to be ineffective.	95%
Diaphragm or cap	Can be put in place before intercourse. Usually no serious side effects.	Spermicide can cause irritation and, in some cases, cystitis (an illness that makes it painful to urinate). Need to learn how to use it correctly.	92–96%

Some couples prefer barrier methods because they are simple to use without the need to plan too far ahead. There are usually no side effects and they are safe to use whilst **breastfeeding**. However, some couples find barrier methods interrupt sex.

Hormonal methods

All hormonal methods of contraception are used by women. Hormonal methods prevent conception through the use of artificial hormones (hormones which are made to be very similar to those produced naturally by the body). Some of them are taken orally (through the mouth) and others are placed or injected into the body. They are free through the NHS.

Contraceptive pills

The combined pill contains artificial versions of the hormones oestrogen and progesterone. It works by stopping the ovary from releasing an egg, so that fertilisation cannot take place. It must be taken at the same time each day to ensure effectiveness. Most types of combined pill are taken every day for 21 days followed by a 7-day gap, during which the woman has a menstrual period. The combined pill is available on prescription from GP surgeries, family planning clinics and sexual health clinics.

The progesterone only pill (POP) does not contain oestrogen. It works by making the mucus in the cervix so thick that the sperm cannot reach the egg. It must be taken at the same time each day to ensure effectiveness. It is taken every day. The POP is available on prescription from GP surgeries, family planning clinics and sexual health clinics. See Table 1.3 for more information (see Figure 1.6).

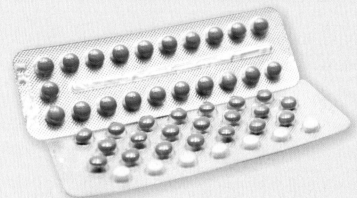

Figure 1.6: Some oral contraceptives are taken daily, whilst others are taken for 21 days followed by a gap of 7 days

Table 1.3: The advantages, disadvantages and effectiveness of oral contraceptive pills

Type of contraceptive pill	Advantages	Disadvantages	Effectiveness when used correctly (Source: NHS)
Combined pill	A woman can start taking the pill at any time during her menstrual cycle but may need additional protection at first. Menstrual periods can become more regular, lighter and less painful. The pill can be used to regulate periods so a woman knows when her period will happen. Can reduce the risk of some health conditions and diseases such as fibroids and ovarian cysts.	May not be effective if a woman is taking medication or if she has sickness or diarrhoea. May increase blood pressure or the likelihood of clots, strokes or breast or cervical cancer. May not be appropriate for all women, for example smokers or those over 35. No protection against sexually transmitted infections (STIs).	Over 99%
POP	Can be used if a woman is unable to use contraception which contains oestrogen. Can be used whilst breastfeeding. Can be used at any age.	May not be effective if a woman is taking medication or if she has sickness or diarrhoea. May not have regular periods. No protection against STIs.	Over 99%

Contraceptive injection

The contraceptive injection prevents pregnancy by releasing progestogen into the bloodstream and preventing ovulation. It also thickens the mucus around the cervix and prevents the sperm from reaching the egg.
The most commonly used injection lasts for 13 weeks. The contraceptive injection is available through a GP surgery or clinic. Women can also learn to inject themselves.

Contraceptive implant

The contraceptive implant is a small rod which is inserted beneath the skin in the arm. The rod contains the hormone progestogen which it releases into the bloodstream to prevent an egg from being released. It lasts for three years. The contraceptive implant is available from family planning clinics, sexual health clinics and some GP surgeries.

Intrauterine device

An **intrauterine** device (IUD) is also sometimes called a coil (see Figure 1.7). It is inserted into the uterus. It prevents pregnancy by releasing copper which alters the cervical mucus and prevents a sperm from reaching an egg. It can also stop a fertilised egg from being able to implant in the uterus lining. It can stay in place for five to ten years. An IUD must be inserted by a trained doctor or nurse, and the woman should check regularly that it is still in place.

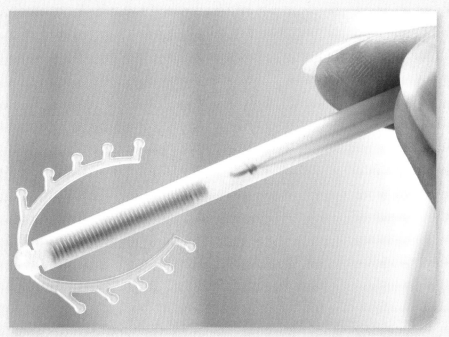

Figure 1.7: An IUD's effectiveness is not reduced by illness or the use of other medicines

Intrauterine system

An intrauterine system (IUS) works in a similar way to an IUD as it is inserted into the uterus by a doctor or nurse. However, the IUS releases progestogen into the system rather than copper to prevent pregnancy. This thickens the mucus around the cervix which makes it difficult for the sperm to reach the egg. In some cases, it also prevents ovulation and menstrual periods may stop after one year.

Emergency contraceptive pill

The emergency contraceptive pill or 'morning after pill' should only be used in cases of unprotected sex. It should be taken within three days and works by stopping or delaying the release of an egg. It is not recommended as a regular form of contraception. The morning after pill is available after a consultation with the woman's GP or through a clinic. See Table 1.4 for more information.

Hormonal methods of contraception are very popular. This is because if they are taken or used correctly they are very effective. Sex can be spontaneous without the need to plan ahead. They can also be used quite soon after having a baby to prevent pregnancy.

In the case of taking the pill, they also mean that women can predict exactly when they are going to menstruate (have a period), or control when this happens. This can be useful, for example if they have a special occasion and do not want to be menstruating (having a period) at that time. Taking the pill can also relieve some symptoms of menstruation, such as severe period pain and premenstrual tension (PMT).

The POP, morning after pill, IUD, IUS and contraceptive implant are all safe to be used whilst breastfeeding, although this is not true of all hormonal methods.

Table 1.4: The advantages, disadvantages and effectiveness of other hormonal methods of contraception

Other types of hormonal methods	Advantages	Disadvantages	Effectiveness when used correctly (Source: NHS)
Contraceptive injection	Lasts up to 13 weeks. Menstrual periods can become more regular, lighter and less painful. Can be used whilst breastfeeding. Not affected by medication.	It can take up to a year for periods to return to normal after injections stop. Can stop periods altogether. May cause weight gain. Side effects may include mood swings and headaches. No protection against STIs.	More than 99%
Contraceptive implant	Can be used if a woman is unable to use contraception which contains oestrogen. Works for three years. Safe to use whilst breastfeeding. Fertility goes back to normal as soon as it's removed.	Periods may become irregular or stop. Some medication may make it less effective. Need a doctor or nurse to have it put in and taken out. No protection against STIs.	More than 99%
IUD	Medication does not interfere with the IUD. Can be fitted four weeks after giving birth. Can be put in at any time during the menstrual cycle and works straight away. No hormonal side effects such as weight gain or headaches. No health risks.	Small risk of infection after it is put in place. Can be uncomfortable for a few months in the beginning. Increased risk of heavier periods. May not be suitable for all women, for example if they have problems with their uterus or cervix. No protection against STIs.	More than 99%
IUS	Works for three to five years. Periods can become more shorter, lighter and less painful. Safe to use when breastfeeding. Not affected by medication.	May cause side effects such as headaches and breast tenderness. May cause mood swings. Some women may develop cysts on their ovaries but this is rare. No protection against STIs.	More than 99%
Emergency contraceptive pill	Can be used after intercourse in cases where a couple has not used other forms of contraception, for example has forgotten to take a pill or if a condom has split. No serious side effects.	Should not be used for contraception on a regular basis. Can cause sickness and headaches. May be less effective for those on some types of medication or who have severe asthma. No protection against STIs.	Effective if taken within three days.

Let's get practical! 3

Use a computer to create an information poster showing the advantages and disadvantages of the different types of hormonal contraception methods.

Natural family planning

Natural family planning (sometimes called fertility awareness) is a method of preventing pregnancy by following the menstrual cycle. The woman learns about her menstrual cycle in three different ways and finds out when she is most fertile and likely to conceive (as conception is more likely on certain days of the month). These are the:

- temperature method
- cervical mucus method
- calendar method.

If no other method of contraception is being used, couples are advised to use all three methods to increase the likelihood of managing their fertility effectively. Generally speaking, women are at their most fertile in the days before ovulation, during ovulation and around 24 hours afterwards. (See Section 1.4.1 for more information on the menstrual cycle.) After ovulation, the egg only lives for 24 hours, so for fertilisation to occur there must be sperm present at that time. Sperm can live for up to seven days.

Temperature method

The temperature method involves a woman taking her temperature every morning at the same time before getting up. After ovulation, a woman's temperature increases slightly for several days.

Cervical mucus method

This method of tracking fertility monitors changes in the mucus secreted by the cervix. When a woman is at her most fertile (at or just before ovulation) the mucus goes from being moist and creamy to being clear and slippery for around three days. After the mucus has stopped being clear the woman is not as fertile for the rest of her cycle.

Calendar method

The calendar method is also often called the rhythm method. It is similar to the temperature method as a woman needs to track her cycle to see when she is most fertile. The woman will look at her cycles over time to estimate when she is likely to be ovulating. See Table 1.5 for more information.

Table 1.5: The advantages, disadvantages and effectiveness of methods of contraception

Method of natural family planning	Advantages	Disadvantages	Effectiveness (Source: NHS)
Temperature method/ cervical mucus method/ calendar method	No side effects. Many religions and cultures accept it as a birth-control method.	Couples can only have sex at certain times of the month if they are using this method to prevent pregnancy. No protection against STIs.	Up to 99%

The natural family planning method has advantages in that it does not use any artificial form of contraception which interferes with the body. However, it can be unreliable if it is not carried out correctly and can be difficult to abstain from having sex.

Natural family planning is sometimes used for religious reasons, for example if the couple's beliefs prevent them from using any artificial form of contraception such as hormonal or barrier methods.

Case study

Marietta and Geoff

Marietta and her husband Geoff have two children and are considering using natural methods of family planning. Marietta is on long-term medication which would reduce the effectiveness of most hormonal methods. They have used barrier methods in the past but find them intrusive. They do not want to have any more children. They have sex regularly.

Figure 1.8: Marietta and Geoff with their children

Check your understanding

1   Why do you think natural methods are a good form of contraception for Marietta and Geoff?

2   Describe the advantages and disadvantages of natural methods of contraception.

3   Evaluate whether these methods are the best choice for Marietta and Geoff.

Over to you! 2

What type of contraceptives are these examples? Copy out the table then tick the correct box.

Type of contraceptive	Barrier	Hormonal	Natural
IUD			
Female condom			
Calendar method			
Contraceptive injection			

1.4 The structure and function of the reproductive systems

Let's get started 3

Look at the list of reproductive parts of the body.
Do you think they are male or female?

testes   **ovary**   **urethra**   **fallopian tube**

The structure and function of the female reproductive system

In order to understand human reproduction, you need to know about the main parts of the female reproductive system and how they work. Figure 1.9 shows the five main parts.

Ovaries

The **ovaries** are the main female reproductive organ. Women have two ovaries, which are found in the lower part of the abdomen. They each contain and release eggs. Female babies are born with all the eggs they

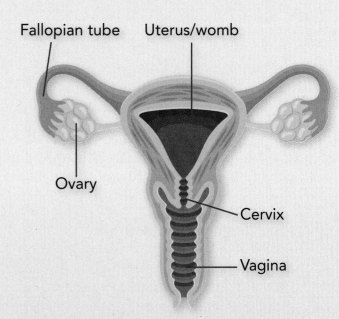

Figure 1.9: The five main parts of the female reproductive system

will need during their lifetime. The ovaries usually release one egg each month. This is called ovulation. (See Section 1.5 for more information about ovulation, conception and fertilisation.)

The ovaries also produce the reproductive hormones **oestrogen** and **progesterone**, which regulate the maturation (age and development) and release of the eggs and maintain the lining of the uterus.

Fallopian tubes

Although they are not directly connected to the ovaries, the **fallopian tubes** carry the released egg from the ovary to the uterus. They also carry male sperm to the egg for fertilisation, which takes place in the fallopian tube around the time of ovulation. The fertilised egg is then carried by the fallopian tubes into the **uterus**, where it implants in (attaches to) the lining.

Uterus/womb

The lining of the uterus (womb) thickens each month in preparation to receive a fertilised egg. If this does not happen, the lining is shed and this passes out through the vagina as a woman's monthly menstrual period.

If fertilisation does occur, the uterus contains, protects and **nourishes** the foetus and placenta whilst they grow and develop during pregnancy. It expands as they grow. Its other function during pregnancy is to remove any waste material which comes from the foetus.

Cervix

The **cervix** is the lower part of the uterus and leads to the top of the vagina. It produces cervical mucus which supports the entry of sperm and protects the internal reproductive organs from bacteria. The cervix opens each month so that blood and tissue can come out of the uterus and into the vagina during menstruation.

Vagina

The **vagina** has several functions as part of the reproductive system. It receives the penis during intercourse and holds the sperm before it passes into the uterus. The vagina also acts as a passageway, both for childbirth and for the release of blood and tissue during menstruation.

The menstrual cycle

The **menstrual cycle** is the monthly process of ovulation and menstruation when a woman's body prepares for the possibility of pregnancy. The cycle takes an average of 28 days. It starts on average around the age of 12 in girls and finishes around the age of 50, when a woman's menstrual periods will gradually stop and she can no longer have children.

The menstrual cycle is controlled by hormones and starts from the first day of a woman's menstrual period and ends on the day before her next one. It contains four phases, which are shown in Figure 1.10:

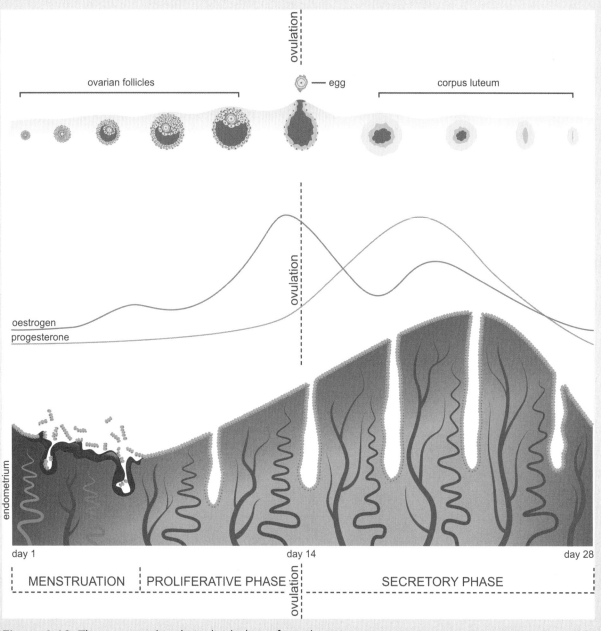

Figure 1.10: The menstrual cycle is divided into four phases.

- **Phase 1, Menstruation:** During the first five days of a woman's menstrual cycle the uterus sheds its lining and the woman menstruates.

- **Phase 2, Proliferative phase:** Over the next nine days, levels of oestrogen and progestogen increase and an egg matures in the ovarian **follicle**. Oestrogen causes the lining of the uterus to start to get thicker. The cervical mucus becomes thinner to allow sperm to reach the egg.

- **Phase 3, Ovulation:** At around day 14 of the cycle, ovulation occurs and oestrogen levels are at their highest. The egg is released from the ovarian follicle and enters the fallopian tube. This is the time when a woman is at her most fertile.

- **Phase 4, Secretory phase:** The ovarian follicle closes after the egg has been released. This produces progesterone which prepares the lining of the uterus for fertilisation. If fertilisation does not take place, levels of progesterone reduce and the body prepares to menstruate. This phase lasts around 14 days.

The structure and function of the male reproductive system

Look at Figure 1.11, which shows the male reproductive system.

Testes

The **testes** (also called testicles) produce and store sperm. They also produce the male sex hormone testosterone. They are located in the scrotum which is a sac of skin behind the penis. The testes are outside the body so that sperm can develop at the optimal temperature, which is slightly cooler than body temperature.

Sperm duct/epididymis

The **sperm duct** or epididymis is a long tube in which the sperm matures and is stored after being produced in the testes. As it matures it is carried from the testes to the **vas deferens**. This is a tube that carries the mature sperm from the sperm duct to the **urethra** before ejaculation.

Urethra

The urethra is a tube which carries urine from the bladder, through the penis and out of the body. During male arousal, a ring of muscle in the urethra closes to prevent urine travelling through it. When a man has an orgasm, the urethra ejaculates sperm out through the penis.

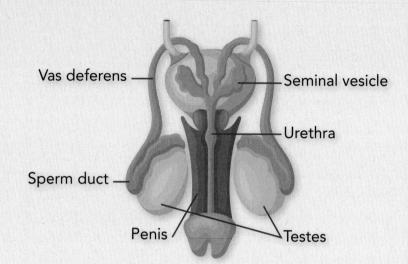

Figure 1.11: The male reproductive system

Penis

The **penis** is the male sexual organ. It becomes erect and enlarges during sexual intercourse when it fills with blood. When this happens it can penetrate into the woman's vagina. The skin of the penis is loose so that it can stretch and enlarge during an erection.

Seminal vesicle

The **seminal vesicle** is one of a pair of glands which are situated each side of the bladder. During ejaculation, the seminal vesicles add fluid and nutrients to the sperm to produce semen.

Test your knowledge   1

1 State the functions of the vagina.

2 Look at the following phases of the menstrual cycle and put them in the correct order:

- Ovulation
- Menstruation
- Secretory phase
- Proliferative phase

3 What is the benefit of the testes being situated outside the body?

4 Look at the following words. Create a list of the male reproductive system terms and a list of the female reproductive system terms.

epididymis   cervix   uterus   urethra   seminal vesicle

1.5 How reproduction takes place

Let's get started   4

How do humans reproduce? What do you know about the process of reproduction and how a baby is formed?

Before starting this section, look back at what you have learnt about the male and female reproductive systems (see Section 1.4). Remember, a couple's pre-conception health will have a significant impact on whether they will be able to conceive (see Section 1.1). You may wish to refer to the menstrual cycle diagram in Figure 1.10. This section looks at the steps leading to reproduction. Each step is driven by hormonal changes.

Ovulation

Ovulation occurs at around day 14 of a woman's menstrual cycle, when one of her ovaries releases a mature egg into one of the fallopian tubes. It is around **ovulation** that a woman is at her most fertile. After the egg has been released, there is a time window of about 12–24 hours in which it can be fertilised by the male sperm. If the egg is not fertilised, it breaks down along with the uterus lining and is released as a menstrual period at the end of the menstrual cycle (see Figure 1.10).

Conception/fertilisation

If sexual intercourse takes place around the time of ovulation, the male sperm may fertilise the female egg. This is known as **conception** or fertilisation. It usually takes place in a fallopian tube.

The sex of the future baby is decided by the sperm. If the sperm contains an X chromosome, the baby will be a girl, but a Y chromosome will mean that the baby is a boy.

Implantation

The lining of the fallopian tube contains tiny hairs, or cilia, which help the fertilised egg to move towards the uterus. The fertilised egg travels through the fallopian tube over the next six to ten days until it reaches the uterus.

The fertilised egg implants into the lining of the uterus. This is known as **implantation**. As it travels through the fallopian tube, the fertilised egg is dividing into cells. After implantation into the uterus, the fertilised egg is known as an **embryo**.

Development of the embryo and foetus

The words 'embryo' and 'foetus' both refer to the baby which is developing inside the woman's uterus. The term 'embryo' is normally used up to and including the eighth week of pregnancy. After this it is known as a **foetus**.

There are many rapid changes in the first few weeks as the embryo starts to grow and develop. Some basic physical features start to appear by the end of the eighth week, including the heart and the neural tube. The limb buds (where the arms and legs will be) start to form. At eight weeks the embryo is still very small – around the size of a lemon.

The embryo is in a sac of liquid called **amniotic fluid**. This has several functions:

- Protection: the fluid helps to protect the developing baby.

- Temperature control: the foetus is insulated and kept at a consistent temperature by the fluid during pregnancy.

- Infection control: the fluid contains antibodies, which reduce the risk of infection to the foetus.

- Muscle/bone development: as the foetus floats in the fluid inside the amniotic sac, its movement in the uterus is supported, allowing it to move freely so that muscles and bones are able to develop.

- Lubrication: the fluid stops some parts of the body from growing together, for example fingers and toes. In cases where the amount of fluid is low, webbing can sometimes occur.

Figure 1.12 shows the functions of amniotic fluid.

The **umbilical cord** develops from the embryo around week 5. It passes nutrients from the placenta to the foetus throughout the rest of the pregnancy.

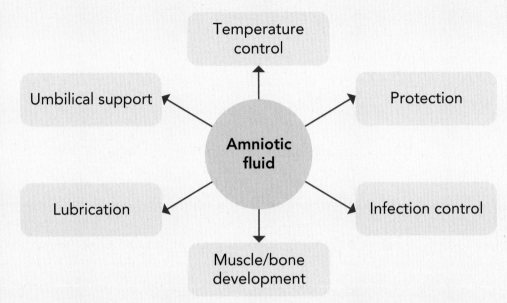

Figure 1.12: The different functions of amniotic fluid

After implantation, the placenta starts to develop from the embryo. It holds the embryo in place in the uterus. The placenta is fully formed by the 12th week but continues to grow throughout the pregnancy. The function of the placenta is to nourish the growing foetus for the remainder of the pregnancy.

Multiple pregnancies

A multiple pregnancy is one in which the mother is carrying more than one baby. According to the Royal College of Obstetricians and Gynaecologists, it occurs in around 1 in 80 pregnancies in the UK. A multiple pregnancy might mean twins, triplets or quadruplets, but one mother gave birth to eight babies – all of whom survived.

A multiple pregnancy may occur for several reasons, due to the different ways in which fertilisation can happen.

Identical (monozygotic) **twins** are formed when one egg is fertilised by one sperm and then splits on fertilisation or shortly afterwards. This means that both sides of the egg produce an embryo which has the same genes. The babies share a placenta and are always the same sex.

Identical twins share many characteristics. It can be difficult to tell some identical twins apart, whilst others may look slightly different, for example one may be bigger than the other.

Look at Figure 1.13. What is the difference between identical and non-identical twins at fertilisation?

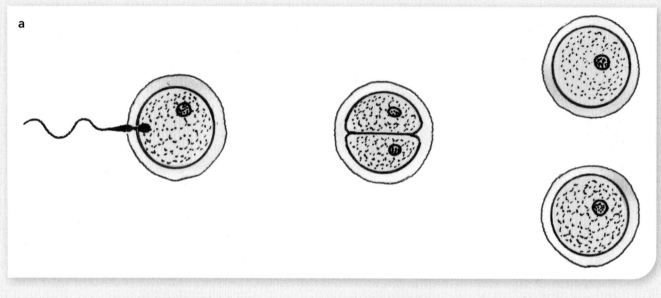

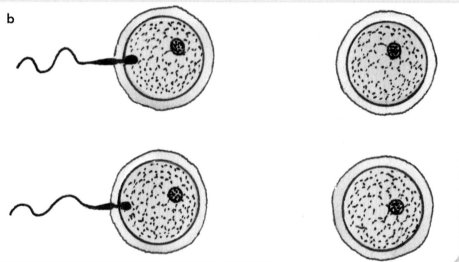

Figure 1.13: a Identical twins at fertilisation; **b** Non-identical twins at fertilisation

Non-identical (fraternal or dizygotic) **twins** are formed when more than one egg is released from a woman's ovaries during ovulation and each egg is fertilised by a different sperm. This means the babies have their own placentas and umbilical cords and are not joined in any way.

Fraternal twins may be two boys, two girls or one of each sex. They will be like any other siblings (brothers and sisters) but will share a birthday.

Sometimes, twins and multiple births run in families, particularly if the mother has a fraternal twin. It is possible for a woman to have several sets of twins.

In a multiple pregnancy, it is likely that the mother will be monitored more closely as there is a higher risk of health complications. Identical twins in particular need to be checked regularly as having a shared placenta means that they also share a blood supply, which can sometimes be unequal.

Multiple pregnancies are more likely to occur in cases where the woman has had IVF. This is because IVF involves fertilising an egg with sperm outside of the woman's body and then putting the fertilised egg (embryo) back into her uterus. To increase the chances that IVF will be successful, more than one embryo is sometimes placed in the woman's body. This can result in a multiple pregnancy (see Figure 1.14).

Figure 1.14: Why might fertility treatment increase the likelihood of having more than one baby?

Over to you!   3

1   Which of the following couples are more likely to conceive more than one baby? Explain why this is the case.

   a   John and Amy, who are both from small families with no multiple births

   b   Zsusana and Maria, who are hoping to conceive a baby through IVF

   c   Miriam and Trevor, who have a set of twins already.

2   Write about the differences between identical and non-identical twins and why they occur.

1.6 The signs and symptoms of pregnancy

Let's get started   5

Why does a woman usually think that she may be pregnant?

When we think about the most common **sign** of pregnancy, we usually think about the woman missing her period. However, there are also other signs and **symptoms** which women may experience during the early stages of pregnancy. Many of these are caused by the hormonal changes which are taking place in the woman's body. Not all symptoms will be experienced by all women (see Figure 1.15).

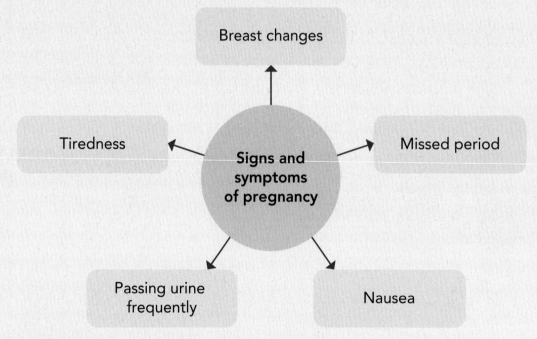

Figure 1.15: Common signs and symptoms of pregnancy

Breast changes

Due to changes in hormone levels, the breasts are likely to feel larger and more uncomfortable in the first few weeks of pregnancy. The nipples may also become darker and stand out more. As the pregnancy progresses, the breasts may feel heavier and more sore.

Missed period

A pregnant woman will stop having periods. This is one of the earliest signs that she is pregnant. She will not have another period until after the baby is born. If there is a small amount of bleeding, this may relate to the fertilised egg being implanted in the uterus as this sometimes causes a small amount of 'spotting'. However, a large amount of bleeding may mean that the woman is having a miscarriage.

Nausea

Nausea (feeling sick) and vomiting (being sick) are common symptoms of early pregnancy. These symptoms are often known as 'morning sickness'. Morning sickness usually starts when the woman is 4 to 6 weeks pregnant and should stop before the 20th week. It can be caused by increased hormone levels or reduced blood sugar, although there is no set reason for it. A woman with severe morning sickness may need additional fluids if she becomes dehydrated. Morning sickness can be worse in multiple pregnancies.

Passing urine frequently

Many women find that they need to pass urine more frequently during the first **trimester** (the first three months of pregnancy). This is caused by an increase in the hormones progesterone and hCG (human chorionic gonadotropin). The need reduces in the second trimester (the next three months of the pregnancy) but increases again towards the end. This is because as the baby grows it puts more pressure on the bladder.

Tiredness

Tiredness is another common symptom of pregnancy, particularly in the first three months. This is also due to hormonal changes. Tiredness is likely to worsen again towards the end of the pregnancy as the woman is carrying more weight and it becomes more difficult to sleep. It is important for a woman to get as much rest as possible.

Review your learning

Test your knowledge 2

1 Draw a spider diagram to show the different functions of amniotic fluid.

2 Copy out and complete the sentences with the words below.

   breasts   morning sickness   six   woman   missed period

   A _____ will notice changes in her body in early pregnancy.
   A _____ may be the earliest sign that she is pregnant.
   Other signs may include _____, which may start from four to
   _____ weeks into her pregnancy, and changes to her _____.

3 How does the umbilical cord support the unborn baby?

What have you learnt?

	See section
• Factors affecting pre-conception health for women and men.	1.1
• Other factors affecting pre-conception health for women.	1.2
• Types of contraception methods and their advantages and disadvantages.	1.3
• The structure and function of the reproductive systems.	1.4
• How reproduction takes place.	1.5
• The signs and symptoms of pregnancy.	1.6

Antenatal care and preparation for birth

Let's get started   1

What do you think the term 'antenatal' means?
What preparations do you think parents need to make before birth?
Why are these preparations important?

Figure 1.16: Antenatal preparations

What will you learn?

- The purpose and importance of antenatal clinics.

- Screening and diagnostic tests.

- The purpose and importance of antenatal (parenting) classes.

- The choices available for delivery.

- The role of the birth partner in supporting the mother through pregnancy and birth.

- The methods of pain relief when in labour.

- The signs that labour has started.

- The three stages of labour and their physiological changes.

- The methods of assisted birth.

2.1 The purpose and importance of antenatal clinics

The meaning of the term 'antenatal'

'Antenatal' is formed from two Latin words: *ante* meaning 'before', and *natal* which means 'birth'. It means the medical care which is given to a woman during pregnancy.

The timing of the first antenatal clinic appointment

A woman usually finds out she is pregnant after missing a period and taking a home pregnancy test. These tests are very reliable. Following a positive pregnancy test, there are two main routes through the NHS to the first antenatal appointment. The woman may see her GP, who may do another pregnancy test, or she may refer herself to her local NHS **antenatal clinic** by filling in an online form early in her pregnancy. These clinics are available at most local hospitals.

> **Over to you!   1**
>
> Find out what information is requested in an online referral form. Search 'maternity self-referral form'.

The online referral form requests health information as well as details of any other pregnancies which the woman may have had. It also triggers the first antenatal appointment, which usually take place between eight and ten weeks of a pregnancy. (The first day of a woman's last period is used to measure how far she is into her pregnancy.) This first antenatal appointment is likely to be the longest and there may be up to nine other appointments. It depends on the number of previous pregnancies or any medical conditions which the woman may have.

Antenatal clinics help to ensure a safe pregnancy and delivery and to prepare a pregnant woman for the birth of her child. They also support the woman's partner or the father of the baby.

The roles of different health professionals

During her pregnancy, a pregnant woman will need to regularly see different health professionals through antenatal appointments, usually at a clinic (see Figure 1.17). This is because it is important to monitor her health and well-being, and the health of her unborn baby, as well as giving her advice and support. It is particularly true in the case of first-time mothers who may need more information and reassurance during pregnancy. Women who do not have regular **antenatal care** are statistically more likely to experience **miscarriage**, stillbirth or have a **premature baby**. According to the baby charity Tommy's, it is estimated that one in four pregnancies still ends in miscarriage or a stillbirth.

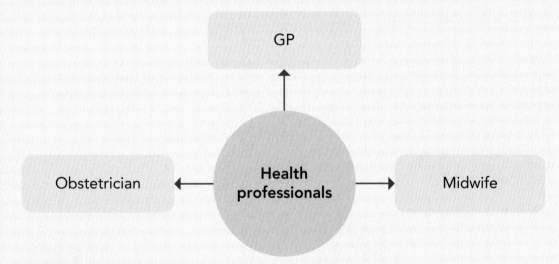

Figure 1.17: Health professionals who support a woman during her pregnancy

Health professionals such as GPs, midwives and obstetricians need to have as much information as possible about a pregnant woman's health and well-being so that they can support her effectively throughout her pregnancy.

GP (General Practitioner)

GPs traditionally had a major role in antenatal care, but this has changed over the last 30 or so years and midwives have taken on more of their responsibilities. However, it is still likely that the GP will be the first health professional a woman visits when she discovers that she is pregnant. This early appointment with the health professional who knows her best is beneficial at the start of a pregnancy. This is because her GP will know a lot about her medical history and any existing health conditions.

The woman may also feel more comfortable talking to her GP than to another health professional. The GP may also be a gateway to other services if they judge that these are needed, for example if the woman or her unborn baby is at risk (see Table 1.6).

Table 1.6: Benefits of a woman's appointment with her GP in early pregnancy

Issue	Benefit
Pre-existing health condition	If a pregnant woman has a pre-existing health condition, her GP will already know about it and will be able to advise at this first appointment if it will have an impact on her pregnancy. The GP will be able to offer advice on what she can do to ensure that her baby is healthy.
Safeguarding and child protection	A pregnant woman may need to be referred to social services if there have been child protection issues in the past, or if the GP has any concerns about her situation. In some cases, pregnancy can be a trigger for domestic abuse or it can make existing domestic abuse worse. This puts the pregnant woman and the baby at risk.
Alcohol/substance abuse	A GP will have information about any history of alcohol or substance abuse. They can discuss this with the woman and refer her for support, if needed, by specialist teams.
Mental health care needs	According to NICE (National Institute for Health and Care Excellence), a pregnant woman should be asked about her mental health the first time she visits her GP during pregnancy and again six weeks after the birth of her baby.
Communication	If there are any issues with communication, for example if the pregnant woman speaks English as an additional language, the GP may recommend to the antenatal clinic that an interpreter or other support is necessary. This will ensure that the woman has access to all the information she needs from the start.

Midwife

A midwife is someone who is specially trained in pregnancy and birth (see Figure 1.18). Midwives have a range of responsibilities. They provide antenatal care such as **clinical examinations** and **screening** for expectant mothers. They also provide care during labour and birth. In addition, they provide **postnatal care** and support for new mothers.

A midwife is likely to develop a good relationship with a pregnant woman as they will see her on a regular basis. They provide emotional support and can answer

Figure 1.18: Why is the role of the midwife so important during pregnancy?

any questions as they arise. They run parenting classes which teach skills such as feeding, bathing and caring for babies, and discuss the birthing options which are available.

Midwives can be based in a hospital unit, GP surgery or antenatal clinic, whilst others work in private care. Community midwives may also carry out home visits. The care and support given by midwives continues for up to a month after the birth of the baby.

Obstetrician

An obstetrician is a doctor who specialises in all aspects of pregnancy and childbirth. They provide medical care to pregnant women both during pregnancy and after the baby is born. An obstetrician will usually be involved if the woman has a health condition or illness themselves, or where there are concerns about the pregnancy. An obstetrician may be present during the birth of the baby in this case or if complications arise during labour. Where there are no issues, a woman will not need to see an obstetrician at all during her pregnancy.

Over to you!   2

What support do the different health professionals give? Copy out the table then put a tick in the correct boxes to show the support each health professional gives.

Health Professional	Provides antenatal care/support	Attends birth	Provides medical care	Provides postnatal care/support
Midwife				
GP				
Obstetrician				

The reasons for routine tests/checks and what conditions they can identify

All pregnant women need to undergo regular routine tests and checks to help to identify a range of conditions which may affect their health or the health of their unborn baby, and to ensure that action is taken where needed (see Table 1.7).

Table 1.7: The problems that routine checks can identify

Type of routine test/check	What it can identify
Baby's heartbeat	This is checked to ensure that the unborn baby is alive and that the heartbeat is normal. (An unborn baby's heartbeat is usually 110–160 beats per minute.)
Blood pressure	The blood pressure of a healthy pregnant woman should be between 110/70 and 120/80. High blood pressure (above 140/90) can be a sign of **pre-eclampsia**.
Blood tests	A pregnant woman's blood is tested to: • check her blood count (check the level of haemoglobin – a protein found in red blood cells) • find out her blood group (A, B, O or AB) • see if she is rhesus negative (as this may mean that the baby is more likely to develop rhesus disease, a condition in which the pregnant woman's body makes antibodies that attack the blood cells of the unborn baby) • check for anaemia, which can make a pregnant woman feel tired because there is not enough iron in her blood • check for infectious diseases such as hepatitis B, HIV or syphilis, as these can affect the health of the pregnant woman and the unborn baby • check for syndromes which may affect the baby including **Down's syndrome**. • check for gestational diabetes if the woman has risk factors such as obesity or polycystic ovary syndrome. Gestational diabetes can cause complications in the pregnancy.
Examination of the uterus	This is usually carried out later in pregnancy from 28 weeks onwards. It involves feeling the sides and top of the woman's abdomen and using a tape measure to measure the size of the uterus. This is to monitor the baby's length. It can identify growth problems in the baby or issues with expected dates.
Urine test	Urine is tested to check for protein, which can be a sign of a urine infection or that the pregnant woman has pre-eclampsia. Urine tests can also be used to check for gestational diabetes if the woman is at risk of developing this.
Weight check	A pregnant woman's weight is tracked and measured over time. Most women gain between 10 and 12.5 kg during pregnancy, most of this after their 20th week. If a woman gains too much weight, it can be a sign of pre-eclampsia or **gestational diabetes**. If she loses weight during pregnancy, it might mean that the baby has stopped growing or that the woman is ill.

Over to you!   3

Match the routine checks (1–5) with the reason why they are carried out (a–e):

1　Examination of the uterus
2　Weight checks
3　Blood pressure
4　Blood tests
5　Baby's heartbeat

a　To check that the baby is alive in the uterus

b　To ensure that the woman is not at risk from pre-eclampsia

c　To check for growth problems and ensure due date is correct

d　To track and measure increase over the pregnancy and check for gestational diabetes or pre-eclampsia

e　To check for anaemia (iron deficiency) and infectious diseases among other things

2.2 Screening and diagnostic tests

The reasons for screening tests and what conditions they can identify

Let's get started   2

Look at the photo. Can you name the test which is being carried out?

Why do you think it is important to undergo different tests during pregnancy?

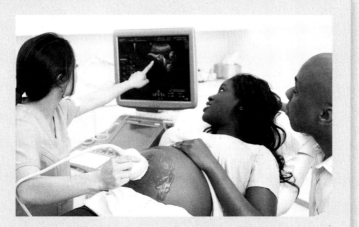

Figure 1.19: Test during pregnancy

Screening tests are offered to all pregnant women, although they do not have to have them. **Screening tests** check the baby's development and identify the risk of specific health problems or conditions. If a risk is identified, the woman may go on to have a **diagnostic test**. A diagnostic test is one used to discover what is wrong and whether a baby has a specific condition. It is important to remember that most babies will develop as expected and there will not be any issues in pregnancy.

Ultrasound scans

Ultrasound scans are taken to gather images of the unborn baby while a woman is pregnant. A sonographer (a health professional who is trained to take ultrasound images) takes the images. They provide information about the baby's growth and development. Under the NHS in England, they are offered at between week 10 and week 14 of pregnancy and again at between week 18 and week 21.

Dating

The first scan at between week 10 and week 14 is important because it checks the unborn baby's size and uses these measurements to work out the estimated date of delivery (due date). The sonographer is also able to find out if there is more than one baby. The dating scan may also include a nuchal fold translucency scan. It is usually possible to find out the sex of the baby at the second scan.

Anomaly

An **anomaly** scan is taken mid-pregnancy, usually at around week 18 to week 21. This test is important because as well as checking the unborn baby's growth and development it looks for signs of 11 rare conditions (see Figure 1.20). It is possible that you may come into contact with a child that has one of these conditions but most of them are very rare.

Open spina bifida is one of the conditions that an anomaly scan can pick up. It is a neural tube defect. It is caused when the spine and spinal cord do not form correctly in early pregnancy. Open spina bifida can be treated with surgery within 48 hours of birth to close the hole, but a child with this condition will have ongoing physical problems such as weakness or loss of sensation in the legs.

According to Great Ormond Street Hospital, a cleft lip affects around 1 in 700 babies in the UK. It happens when parts of the upper lip do not form correctly in pregnancy. It can mean that the baby has trouble feeding because they have problems forming a seal with their lips. Treatment is through surgery when a baby is three to six months old.

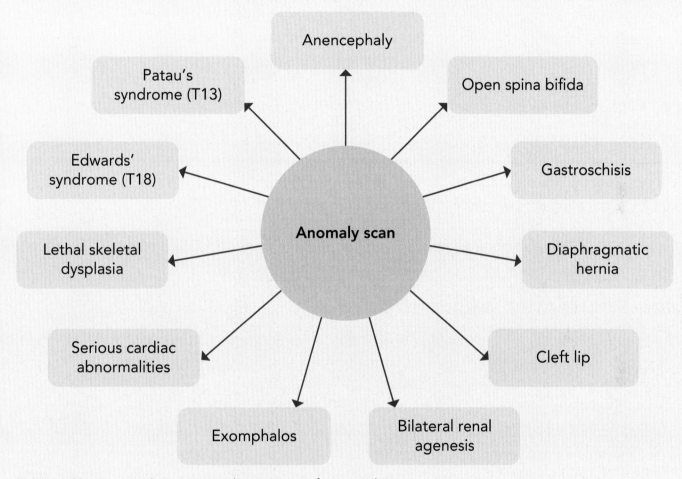

Figure 1.20: An anomaly scan can pick up a range of rare conditions

Nuchal fold translucency scan

This scan usually takes place between week 11 and week 14. It measures the amount of fluid under the skin at the back of the unborn baby's neck. It is used to help to screen for Down's syndrome, as babies with this condition often have more fluid here. It is offered to all pregnant women, although the chance of having a baby with Down's syndrome increases as a woman gets older.

Triple test

The triple test is a blood test which may be offered if the expectant mother is more than 14 weeks pregnant at the time of her first scan. This is another test for Down's syndrome. It is called a triple test because it measures three substances in the blood. This screening test will only identify around 80 percent of babies with the condition, so other tests may be done as well.

Non-Invasive Prenatal Testing (NIPT)

NIPT is another screening test which can be carried out to test for certain genetic abnormalities, such as Down's syndrome (T21), Edwards' syndrome (T18), Patau's syndrome (T13) and some additional chromosomal disorders. It can take place from the tenth week up until the end of pregnancy. Unlike amniocentesis or chorionic villus sampling (CVS), it carries no risk of miscarriage.

The reasons for diagnostic tests and what conditions they can identify

While screening tests can identify that there is a high risk of some conditions, they are not able to confirm them in every case. Diagnostic tests are different from screening tests because they are used to discover what is wrong and whether a baby has a specific condition. In some cases, if the condition is serious or the baby will not survive, this may lead the parents to decide whether or not to continue with the pregnancy.

Amniocentesis

An amniocentesis may be done to test for chromosomal conditions such as Down's syndrome (T21), Edwards' syndrome (T18), Patau's syndrome (T13) or if there is a family history of conditions such as cystic fibrosis, sickle cell disease, thalassaemia (an inherited condition that affects the blood) or muscular dystrophy (a condition which causes the muscles to become weaker over time). In this test, a sample of amniotic fluid is taken from around the baby. This takes place at around 15 weeks of pregnancy and carries some risk of miscarriage.

Chorionic villus sampling (CVS)

A CVS test is also used to test for genetic conditions such as cystic fibrosis, sickle cell disease, thalassaemia or muscular dystrophy. It also tests for chromosomal conditions such as Down's syndrome (T21), Edwards' syndrome (T18) or Patau's syndrome (T13). This test is done between week 11 and week 14 of pregnancy. It involves taking a sample from the placenta after a local **anaesthetic**. Like amniocentesis, it carries some risk to the baby and, according to Tommy's, around a 1 in 100 chance of miscarriage.

Timeline

Figure 1.21 shows a timeline of the tests carried out during pregnancy. In addition, the following checks are offered throughout pregnancy: blood pressure, urine checks, blood tests, weight checks, baby's heartbeat.

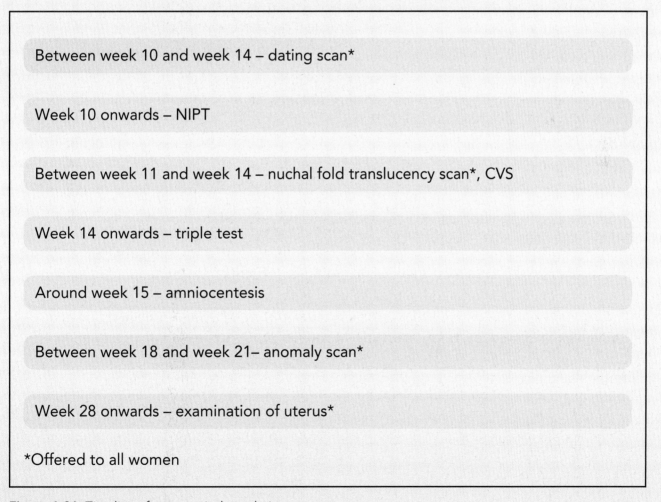

Between week 10 and week 14 – dating scan*

Week 10 onwards – NIPT

Between week 11 and week 14 – nuchal fold translucency scan*, CVS

Week 14 onwards – triple test

Around week 15 – amniocentesis

Between week 18 and week 21– anomaly scan*

Week 28 onwards – examination of uterus*

*Offered to all women

Figure 1.21: Timeline of tests carried out during pregnancy

Test your knowledge   1

1   Sarah is pregnant and going for her first ultrasound scan. List the information the sonographer might be able to find out.

2   Make a table to show whether the following tests are screening or diagnostic: NIPT, amniocentesis, dating scan, triple test, CVS.

3   When might the triple test be offered to a pregnant woman?

2.3 The purpose and importance of antenatal (parenting) classes

Let's get started   3

What do you think antenatal classes are for? Do you think both partners should attend?

Prepares both parents for labour and parenthood

Antenatal classes are offered through both the NHS and private providers and are a good way of preparing for the birth of a new baby (see Figure 1.22). They can be very helpful, particularly for new parents, as they provide information about some of the different aspects of pregnancy and childbirth. Antenatal classes also give parents the opportunity to meet others in their area who are due to give birth at around the same time.

Antenatal classes usually start around week 30. However, parents of twins, triplets and other multiples may start classes earlier as their babies are more likely to be born early.

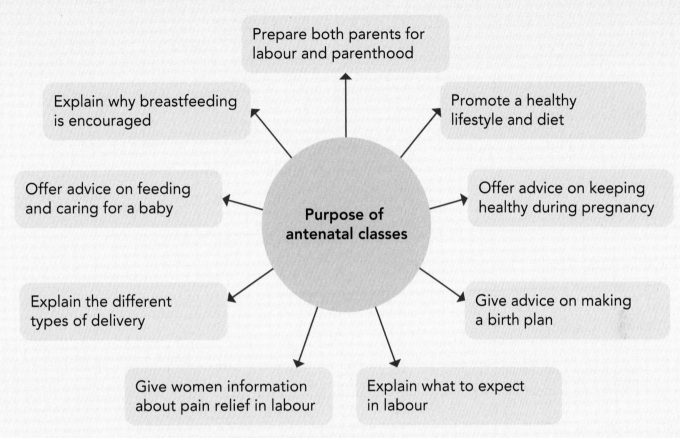

Figure 1.22: Antenatal classes cover a wide range of topics

Promotes healthy lifestyle and diet

One aspect of pregnancy care which is discussed at antenatal classes is a healthy lifestyle and diet. It is important that pregnant women think about eating foods which give the right **nutrients** for the developing baby during pregnancy as well as after birth if they are breastfeeding. It is also a good idea to consider other areas in which they might have a healthier lifestyle, for example if they smoke or drink alcohol, they should stop. This is because having a healthy diet and lifestyle will help both their health and the health of the baby.

Food to avoid during pregnancy

Women should avoid certain foods during pregnancy. Pregnant women should know about these so that they can ensure the safety of their unborn baby (see Table 1.8).

At least five portions of fruit, vegetables and salad should be eaten every day as part of a healthy diet, but it is very important that they are washed thoroughly as any soil residue can cause illness.

Table 1.8: Foods to avoid in pregnancy

Foods to avoid	Reasons why
Soft cheeses	These are made with unpasteurised milk which may contain listeria. This can cause an infection called **listeriosis** which may lead to miscarriage or stillbirth. It can also damage the health of the baby.
Raw or cured meat such as bacon, pepperoni, salami	**Toxoplasmosis** is an infection which is caused by parasites which may be present in meat. It can cause miscarriage. There is a risk of toxoplasmosis from eating raw and undercooked meat as cooking destroys the parasites. Cured meat has not been cooked.
Liver products	Liver and liver products such as pâté or liver sausage contain vitamin A which can cause harm to an unborn baby.
Raw or partially cooked eggs, unless they are British Lion stamped.	British Lion eggs are less likely to contain **salmonella**, a type of bacteria which can cause food poisoning, because they have been produced under a strict code of practice.
Some types of fish such as raw shellfish	They can have bacteria in them which are harmful and can cause food poisoning.
Oily fish, for example salmon or mackerel	No more than two portions of oily fish should be eaten each week. This is because they can contain pollutants which can harm the unborn baby.
Alcohol	Alcohol can cause long-term damage to the unborn baby. It should also be avoided if planning a pregnancy.
Caffeine	Intake should be kept to a minimum (no more than 200 mg per day) as high levels of caffeine have been linked to low birth weight, miscarriage and stillborn babies.

Over to you!   **4**

Plan a three-course meal for four people, including a friend who is pregnant. Write down your initial thoughts, including the foods you have decided not to serve, and explain why you have made your final choices.

Provides advice on feeding and caring for the baby

Antenatal classes also provide advice on feeding and caring for the baby in the first few weeks and months. This includes how to wash and bathe the baby, how to change a nappy, and also the subject of breastfeeding. Although it sounds straightforward, breastfeeding can present challenges. New parents need advice on:

- how to position the baby and attach to the breast

- how to express milk and keep it for later

- what to do if they have problems such as sore nipples or mastitis (a painful breast infection which can develop during breastfeeding).

Why breastfeeding is encouraged for at least the first two weeks

Although it is not always possible to breastfeed, it is encouraged for those women who can do so for at least the first two weeks as there are several benefits.

The first milk which comes into the breast is called colostrum. It contains very concentrated nutrients which help to build up the baby's immune system. It also contains antibodies to help fight bacteria and viruses. Breast milk also adapts to meet the baby's needs as they grow.

Breastfeeding has long-term benefits for the baby's health, as it can reduce the risk of stomach upsets and **SIDS** (sudden infant death syndrome). When the baby is older it can also reduce the risk of obesity and cardiovascular disease.

Breastfeeding has health benefits for the woman, including lowering the risk of some cancers, obesity and osteoporosis (weak bones).

Breastfeeding is a time of bonding between the mother and baby: this is important as it is a way of spending time together and getting to know each other.

2.4 The choices available for delivery

When planning the delivery of a baby, parents have the choice of either a hospital or a home birth. Each has advantages and disadvantages, and their choice may depend on different factors, such as the health needs of the expectant mother and the baby and whether specialists need to be present.

Hospital birth

Most parents have a hospital birth, particularly in the case of their first baby. This is because they know that the expectant mother and baby will have access to more medical care and pain relief during the birth. New parents are encouraged to have a hospital birth, as are those who may have complications or need specialist support.

Some advantages of a hospital birth:

- A range of trained staff and equipment are available if necessary.
- A wide range of pain relief is available.
- Specialists in neonatal (newborn) care are available.
- The mother may spend longer resting after the birth.
- Round-the-clock care for mother and baby is provided.

Some disadvantages of a hospital birth:

- Some women find it more stressful to be in an unfamiliar hospital environment.
- The mother may have a different midwife than she has had during pregnancy.
- Those present at the birth, the number of visitors and visiting times may be restricted.

Home birth

Parents may decide to have a home birth if both the expectant mother and baby are well and there are no complications. If the woman has had children before and is confident and happy to give birth at home, it can be a more relaxing environment for her. According to the NHS, around 1 mother in 50 gives birth at home in England and Wales.

Some advantages of a home birth:

- The parents' surroundings are familiar and comfortable.
- They do not have to travel to hospital while in labour.
- Other members of the family may be present.
- Most forms of pain relief are available at home.
- The mother might feel more relaxed in her own home and will not have to be separated from her partner after the birth.
- There is no risk of catching a hospital-based infection.
- The mother is more likely to be with a midwife whom she knows.

Some disadvantages of a home birth:

- If there are any problems, help will take longer to arrive.
- It may be necessary to transfer to a hospital during labour.

- The NHS does not recommend home birth for first pregnancies, as it may put the baby at greater risk.

- **Epidurals** cannot be given at home.

- The mother may be less likely to rest after the birth.

- It is not recommended for every type of pregnancy, for example multiple pregnancies or if the baby is breech (lying feet first).

2.5 The role of the birth partner in supporting the mother through pregnancy and birth

A birth partner is someone who is nominated (chosen) by a pregnant woman to give her physical and emotional support both before and during the birth of her baby. A birth partner is a valuable form of reassurance and comfort, particularly during labour and birth. The birth partner may be the baby's father, but it may also be a friend or close relative, and in some cases may be more than one person.

A birth partner should be positive and calm and be able to provide support and encouragement throughout the process. According to Tommy's baby charity, those women who have support from a birth partner are likely to find the experience of labour and birth a more positive one. It is also good for the well-being and safety of the woman and her baby.

The benefits of having a birth partner can include:

- to help make the birth plan

- physical and emotional support

- to explain what is happening during labour

- to speak on the pregnant woman's behalf.

Physical support

Physical support primarily involves being present with the woman during labour and birth. This may mean rubbing her back, holding her hand or helping her to move about when she needs to do so. The birth partner may also attend some antenatal classes, and additional support may involve helping the woman with relaxation or reminding her of breathing techniques which she has learnt. If the birth is at home, the birth partner may also have a practical role such as getting things as they are needed (for example, a warm pad to help the pregnant woman feel more relaxed) or supporting her with pain relief.

Emotional support

The birth partner provides emotional support throughout the pregnancy.

Birth partners can talk through the **birth plan** with the woman and her midwife and discuss options such as whether she should have a home or hospital birth. They may also talk about issues such as the woman's preferred type of pain relief, and what kind of support she may need during labour. The birth plan is usually written down and used during labour, although the woman can change it at any time.

The emotional support of a birth partner is particularly important during labour and birth (see Figure 1.23). The birth partner is able to provide this because they know the woman well and are aware of the birth plan. They also provide company and support as labour progresses and the woman's **contractions** become stronger. Giving reassurance, encouragement and praise during labour and birth is an important part of emotional support as it helps to reduce anxiety.

Figure 1.23: A birth partner providing support in the onset of labour

The birth partner will talk to the woman during labour and birth, for example telling them what is happening and passing on information if needed. They may also remind her about aspects of labour that they have learnt about in antenatal classes.

Sometimes during labour, the woman may not feel able to speak out about her wishes. In this situation, she may feel more comfortable in asking her birth partner to do so for her. If an intervention is needed such as **assisted birth** or a **caesarean section**, she may need to ask her birth partner to ask for more information. (For more information about assisted birth see Section 2.9.)

2.6 The methods of pain relief when in labour

Women may be offered different types of pain relief when they are in labour. It is important for them to know in advance what is available and what may be best for them.

Epidural anaesthetic

An epidural is a type of anaesthetic given by an anaesthetist, so it is only available in hospital. The anaesthetist will administer it through a needle in the back so that pain relief can be given at different times during labour and childbirth. An epidural is highly effective in relieving pain and can be used if labour is particularly long or painful. It is also sometimes used where the mother needs to have a caesarean section (see Section 2.9), as it means that she can be awake when her baby is born.

An epidural works by numbing the nerves which carry pain impulses from the birth canal to the brain. As it takes around 20–30 minutes to take effect and a few hours to wear off, it needs to be given by the anaesthetist at the correct time.

See Table 1.9 for the advantages and disadvantages of epidural anaesthetic as a method of pain relief when in labour.

Table 1.9: Advantages and disadvantages of an epidural anaesthetic

Advantages	Disadvantages
• Gives complete pain relief in most cases. • Can be awake during a caesarean section. • Pain relief can be topped up when needed.	• Can cause blood pressure to drop leading to feelings of light-headedness. • Can prolong the second stage of labour as contractions cannot be felt as easily. • May also cause the legs to feel numb. • May cause sickness and headaches. • Can cause difficulties in passing urine.

Gas and air (Entonox)

Gas and air is a mixture of oxygen and nitrous oxide gas. It is breathed in through a mask that is held by the pregnant woman so she can control when she takes it. Gas and air takes around 15–20 seconds to work so it should be breathed in at the start of a contraction.

See Table 1.10 for the advantages and disadvantages of gas and air as a method of pain relief when in labour.

Table 1.10: Advantages and disadvantages of gas and air

Advantages	Disadvantages
• Can be controlled by the woman. • No harmful side effects for mother or baby. • Easy to use.	• Can cause feelings of light-headedness and/or drowsiness. • Can cause sickness. • May need additional pain relief.

Pethidine

Pethidine is an injection which is given in the thigh or buttock. Its effects last for between two and four hours, so it should be given in the early stages of labour.

See Table 1.11 for the advantages and disadvantages of pethidine as a method of pain relief when in labour.

Table 1.11: Advantages and disadvantages of pethidine

Advantages	Disadvantages
• Most effective during the first stage of labour (see Section 2.8). • Can help the woman to relax as well as relieving pain.	• Should not be given too close to the second stage of labour as it can affect the woman's ability to push during labour. • Can affect the baby's breathing if given too close to delivery. • Can interfere with the baby's first feed. • Can cause sickness in the woman.

TENS

TENS stands for transcutaneous electrical nerve stimulation. This method of pain relief involves using a mild electric current which is attached to the woman's skin (in labour this is on her back) using sticky pads. The electrical impulses block the transmission of pain to the brain. A TENS machine is controlled using a handheld device and is usually used in the early stages of labour. It can be used at home or in hospital.

See Table 1.12 for the advantages and disadvantages of TENS as a method of pain relief when in labour.

Table 1.12: Advantages and disadvantages of TENS

Advantages	Disadvantages
• Can be controlled by the woman. • Can be used with Entonox or pethidine. • Easy to stop use immediately if other methods are preferred. • Can reduce anxiety. • No side effects.	• Some women do not like the sensation. • There is limited research about its effectiveness. • Not suitable for use in the more active stages of labour during stronger contractions.

Test your knowledge   2

1   Which of these topics might be covered in antenatal classes?

what happens in labour   **types of pain relief available**
when you should go to hospital   **foods to avoid in pregnancy**

2   Are the following statements true or false?

• Home births are encouraged for a first baby.

• Breastfeeding has health benefits for the woman as well as the baby.

• A birth partner will know about the woman's birth plan.

• An epidural anaesthetic takes effect immediately.

2.7 The signs that labour has started

There are several signs which show that **labour** has started. However, not all pregnant women will experience all of them.

A show

A **show** means that some mucus has come away from the entrance to the cervix and passed through the vagina. This will usually look pink and sticky, but there will not be a lot of blood. Having a show of mucus means that the cervix has begun to open, releasing the plug of mucus at the entrance. Labour may follow quickly, but in some cases it may still take a few days. Not all women have a show at the start of labour.

Waters breaking

When we say someone's **waters** have broken, we are referring to the fluid which surrounds the baby in the amniotic sac breaking away. During or just before labour, these fluids may break out of the sac on their own, but in some cases the midwife may break them if the woman is already in labour. There may be a lot of water or just a small amount. If the waters have broken, the mother should go to hospital as there is a risk of infection for the baby.

Contractions start

As labour starts, women experience contractions which will gradually become stronger. A contraction happens when the muscles of the uterus become tighter and then relax. At the start of labour, it may be hard to tell that they are contractions, but they become more intense as labour progresses. They are sometimes accompanied by pains in the back, or pains which are similar to period pains.

2.8 The three stages of labour and their physiological changes

We often talk about three stages of labour. Giving birth is different for all women, but they all pass through the same **physiological** stages. However, each stage may last for a different length of time and women may feel discomfort in different ways.

Stage 1: Neck of the uterus opens

This is the longest stage of labour and is called the latent stage. During this stage, the cervix is softening and gradually opening, ready for the birth of the baby (see Figure 1.24). This process may take a long time: in a first baby, it is usually around 8 to 12 hours and can be longer, but this may happen more quickly with second and subsequent pregnancies (around 5 hours). A woman may have a

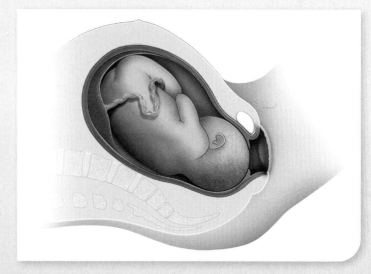

Figure 1.24: Stage 1 of labour

bath or massage at this stage to help with pain relief and moving around may help. If labour is progressing very slowly, or the contractions are not coming often enough, the midwife may talk to the woman about speeding up labour by breaking her waters or putting her on a drip to make her contractions stronger. The first stage of labour finishes when the cervix is fully dilated or open (this is around 10 cm).

Stage 2: Birth of the baby

This stage begins when the cervix is fully dilated and ends when the baby is born. During this stage, the contractions will get closer together and more intense, and the baby will start to move into the birth canal through the vagina and the open cervix (see Figure 1.25). As the contractions are stronger and closer together, the woman will feel the urge to push with each one. This will help to move the baby down the birth canal. It is very tiring, so it is important for her to try to rest between each contraction. This pushing phase may last around three hours with a first baby but not

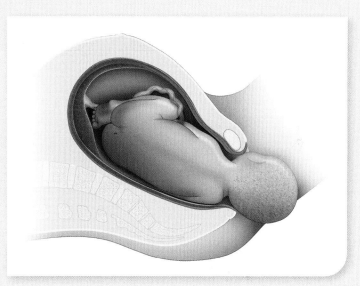

Figure 1.25: Stage 2 of labour

longer than two if the woman has had a baby before. When the head of the baby reaches the entrance to the vagina, the woman will be asked to stop pushing to allow the baby's head to be born more slowly.

A baby will usually be born head first, although some babies are born feet first. This is known as a breech presentation.

Stage 3: Delivery of the placenta

After the baby is born, the third stage of labour is the delivery of the placenta. This can be managed in two different ways. The woman is likely to have discussed this with her midwife and birth partner to tell them how she would prefer this to happen.

The first method is called active management. If the woman has chosen this method, the midwife gives her an injection in her thigh very soon after she has given birth. The injection contains oxytocin, which makes the womb contract (get smaller). This speeds up the process, although as the womb contracts more quickly it may be more painful.

The midwife cuts the umbilical cord between one and five minutes after the birth of the baby. After this, the placenta comes away from the womb. Around 30 minutes after the birth of the baby the midwife gently pulls the umbilical cord so that the placenta is delivered through the vagina.

The second method is called physiological management. This means that the placenta is born without any help to speed it up. After the umbilical cord is cut, the placenta will come away from the womb and the woman will feel the need to push it out. This can take up to an hour in total, although it does not take long to push the placenta out. If the process seems to be taking longer, or if there is any heavy bleeding, the midwife may decide to give an injection to actively manage the third stage (see Figure 1.26).

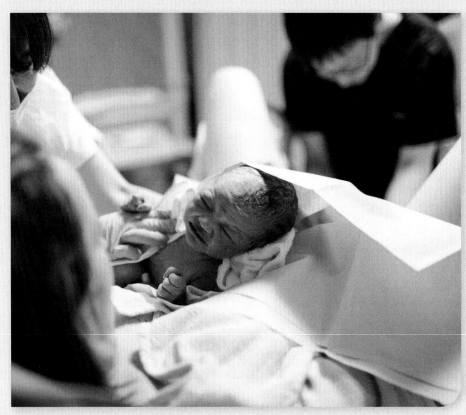

Figure 1.26: What are the two methods of managing the third stage of labour?

2.9 The methods of assisted birth

Assisted birth or instrumental delivery may need to be carried out in situations where help is needed to deliver the baby. It may be planned in advance or become necessary during labour, for example if the baby becomes distressed or the woman has been in labour for a long time and is tired. It is normally used in cases where she has not had a baby vaginally (through the vagina) before. Most methods of assisted birth can only be carried out in a hospital by an obstetrician, and consent will be needed from the woman.

Forceps

Forceps are a medical instrument which look similar to a pair of tongs (see Figure 1.27). They have a curved top which fits around the head of the baby. A forceps delivery may be used by an obstetrician to deliver a baby because:

• the baby is in an awkward position

• the baby has an increased or decreased heart rate

• the woman is not able to push.

As a contraction takes place, the obstetrician guides the baby's head using the forceps and gently pulls to help with delivery. There is some risk of vaginal tearing with forceps delivery.

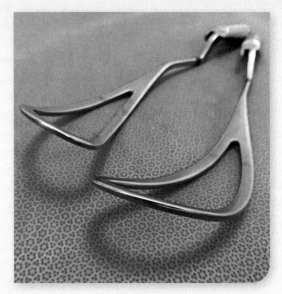

Figure 1.27: In some cases, forceps may be needed to help with the baby's delivery

Ventouse

A **ventouse** is a type of suction cup which is attached to the baby's head. As the woman has a contraction, the obstetrician gently pulls to help with delivery. A ventouse delivery may leave a mark or bruise on the baby's head, as it is very soft before birth, although this will disappear after around two days. A ventouse is not used with very premature babies (less than 36 weeks) as the baby's head is too soft to use it safely.

Episiotomy

In an episiotomy, a small cut is made between the woman's vagina and perineum (anus) to help the baby's head come out. This may happen because:

• the baby's head is too large to fit through the entrance to the vagina easily

• there is going to be a forceps or ventouse delivery

• there is a risk of a tear

• the baby becomes distressed.

After an episiotomy, the area will be stitched with dissolvable stitches.

Elective/emergency caesarean section

A caesarean section is an operation in which the baby is delivered by cutting through the wall of the uterus and lower abdomen (tummy). It is a major operation, so should only be done when needed due to the risks involved. In many cases, the woman will be awake during the birth as she will be able to have an epidural (see Section 2.6). However, this may not be possible if she needs to have an emergency caesarean section.

An elective or planned caesarean section may take place if medical teams know in advance that it is needed. There are number of reasons for this:

- The baby is breech (feet first) and cannot be turned.
- It is a multiple pregnancy and the first baby is breech or lying sideways.
- It is a multiple pregnancy and the babies share a placenta.
- The placenta is low lying (**placenta praevia**).

According to the NHS, in the UK more than half of twins and almost all triplets are delivered by caesarean section.

An emergency caesarean section may take place if a situation arises in which the health of the woman or baby is at risk, and a vaginal delivery becomes unsafe. These are some examples of reasons why an emergency caesarean may take place:

- The woman develops pre-eclampsia (high blood pressure in pregnancy).
- The baby is not getting enough oxygen and needs to be born immediately.
- The labour is not progressing.
- The woman is bleeding heavily.

Case study

Moira

Moira is in labour with her first baby. She is with her birth partner in hospital and her labour has been progressing well. However, she has been told that she may need to have an assisted birth as the baby is in the breech position. She has asked the midwife what types of pain relief might be available.

Check your understanding

1   Describe the different types of assisted birth and which might be used in this case.

2   Identify the most appropriate form of pain relief for Moira.

3   Justify your choice of pain relief.

Review your learning

Test your knowledge   3

1   Which of these signs show that labour has started?

- Feeling sick

- Waters breaking

- A show

- Wanting to push

- Contractions starting

2   Copy out the words and definitions. Match each word to the correct definition.

a	Placenta	high blood pressure in pregnancy
b	Contraction	a small cut which is made between the vagina and perineum
c	Episiotomy	an organ which provides oxygen and nutrients to the foetus through the umbilical cord
d	Pre-eclampsia	a tightening of the muscles of the uterus

What have you learnt?

	See section
• The purpose and importance of antenatal clinics.	2.1
• Screening and diagnostic tests.	2.2
• The purpose and importance of antenatal (parenting) classes.	2.3
• The choices available for delivery.	2.4
• The role of the birth partner in supporting the mother through pregnancy and birth.	2.5
• The methods of pain relief when in labour.	2.6
• The signs that labour has started.	2.7
• The three stages of labour and their physiological changes.	2.8
• The methods of assisted birth.	2.9

TA3

Postnatal checks, postnatal care and the conditions for development

Let's get started   1

Why are postnatal (after birth) checks and continuing care for the mother and baby important? How do you think health professionals might observe and check (monitor) their progress over time?

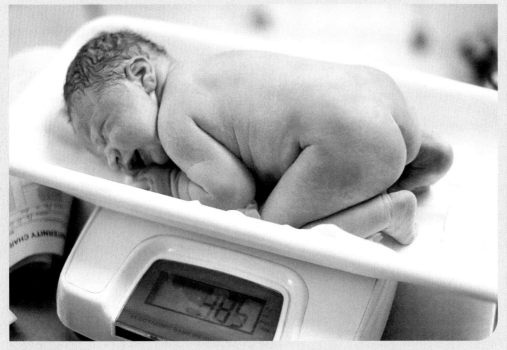

Figure 1.28: Postnatal check

What will you learn?

- Postnatal checks.
- Postnatal care of the mother and baby.
- The developmental needs of children from birth to five years.

3.1 Postnatal checks

Postnatal checks that are carried out on the baby

After the birth of the baby, health professionals immediately carry out a number of different checks to ensure that the baby is healthy and that there are no obvious concerns (see Figure 1.29).

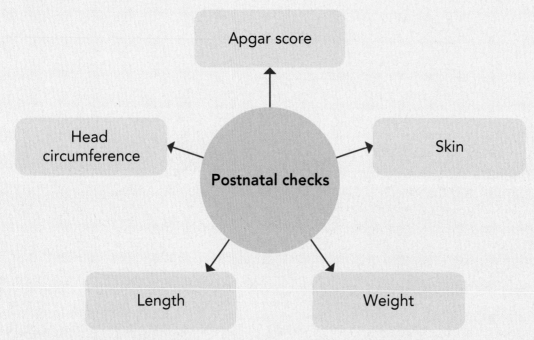

Figure 1.29: Health professionals' physical checks on a newborn baby

Apgar score

A newborn baby is given an Apgar score one minute after birth to evaluate (look at) its physical condition. The score is based on a simple check of the baby's five vital signs (the key things that a health professional checks to see if the baby is healthy, such as how fast their heart is beating and whether they are breathing successfully). 'Apgar' is an acronym of the five different checks (see Table 1.13).

An Apgar score is out of ten as each sign is scored between 0 and 2. In most cases, a healthy baby will have an Apgar score of nine. If, at one minute after birth, some of the baby's vital signs are low, this is less of a concern as they will often pick up in the first few minutes. Some conditions may also cause scores to be lower, such as a difficult or premature birth, but this is likely to be temporary.

Table 1.13: Apgar scores

Check	Score of 0	Score of 1	Score of 2
Appearance (skin)	Whole body looks pale or lacks colour.	Good colour in most of the body but with bluish hands or feet.	Good colour in all areas.
Pulse (heart rate)	None	Slow	Fast
Grimace (makes a face when stimulated (touched) to create a reflex response)	No response when stimulated.	Makes a face when stimulated.	Crying/ coughing
Activity (movement)	Floppy or limp	Some movement/stretching	Greater activity
Respiration (breathing)	None	Weak	Good

When checking appearance in babies with darker skin, it may be harder to assess if they are pale or blue. In this case the doctor or midwife may check the colour of the baby's nail beds, tongue or mouth, or the soles of their feet or palms of their hands.

The Apgar test is repeated five minutes after birth. If the score is six or under and there are concerns, a paediatrician (a doctor who specialises in the care of babies and children) will be informed and the test will be repeated every five minutes.

Over to you! 1

Look at the following Apgar test results. The test has been taken one minute after the baby's birth. What would be the right course of action after this test?

Apgar score	1 minute	5 minutes	10 minutes	15 minutes	20 minutes
Appearance	1				
Pulse	1				
Grimace	1				
Activity	0				
Respiration	1				

In the first few days after birth, the midwife or health visitor carries out further physical tests (see next section).

Skin

Health professionals also look at the baby's skin, which is very thin and can be damaged easily. It can take around a month after birth for the skin to develop a more protective barrier. It is also important to check for any birthmarks or spots which the baby may have, and to look at **vernix** and **lanugo**.

Vernix is a white waxy protective substance which covers the baby's skin while it is in the womb. Its purpose is to help protect the baby from infections and help the baby's skin to retain moisture. Although it is visible on the baby after birth, it is soon absorbed into the skin.

When a baby is overdue (born after its due date), this absorption may happen while still in the womb, so the skin of overdue babies may have a cracked or dry appearance. This peels off in the first few days and the skin beneath is healthy.

Lanugo is a type of soft, fine hair covering. It develops on the baby's body at around the 22nd week of pregnancy and is thought to help keep the baby's body at the right temperature. Lanugo helps the vernix to bind to the baby's skin.

Lanugo is usually shed between the seventh and eighth months of pregnancy although it may still be present on a newborn baby. If this is the case, it disappears in the first few weeks.

Health professionals also check for birthmarks (see Table 1.14). Many of these will disappear over time although they may need to be monitored or treated.

Weight

The baby is weighed at birth and then at regular intervals. This is to ensure that there is a weight gain over time and to check that the baby is growing and developing normally. It also indicates (shows) that the baby is feeding well. The baby's weight is recorded and checked against a **centile chart**, to look at its progress against expected developmental milestones. There are centile charts for boys and girls. See Figure 1.30 for an example of a centile chart for weight for boys aged 0 to 1 year.

Table 1.14: Types of birthmarks

Name	Description
Strawberry marks (infantile haemangiomas)	Strawberry marks are raised, red marks which can be anywhere on the baby's body. They are likely to grow during the first six months but usually disappear on their own in the first few years. They may need treatment or removal if they affect the baby's vision, breathing or feeding.
Flat brown patches (café au lait spots)	These are light or dark patches which may be anywhere on the body. They are common and will look darker on dark skin. If the baby has a large number, this may need to be investigated.
Salmon patches (stork marks)	Salmon patches are flat pink or red patches of skin which are common after birth. They usually appear on the baby's head or neck and fade over time.
Black or brown moles (congenital moles)	These moles are caused by an overgrowth of pigment in the skin. They appear darker on dark skin. Congenital moles should be monitored for any growth as there is a skin cancer risk in this case.

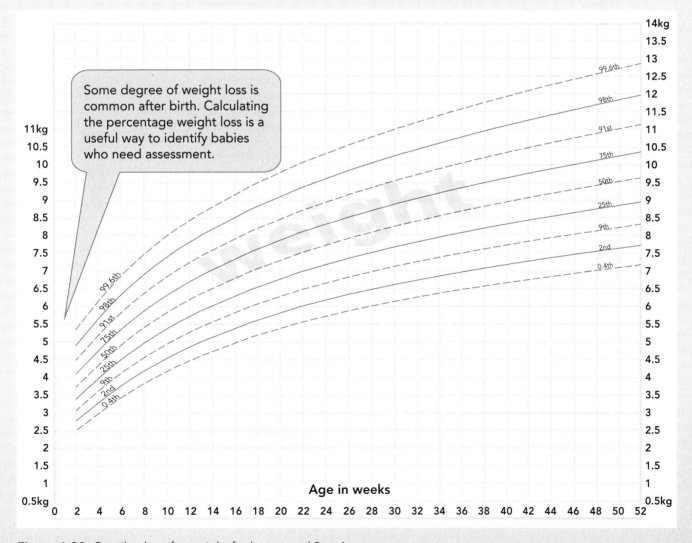

Figure 1.30: Centile chart for weight for boys aged 0 to 1 year

Length

The baby's length is measured at birth to enable health professionals to monitor its growth. Length is tracked on a centile chart in the same way as weight. A newborn baby is usually between 50 and 53 cm long.

Head circumference

Health professionals also look at the shape of the baby's head. It may look squashed after birth but this is normal and changes over time. The **circumference** of the baby's head is measured and then tracked on a centile chart to check brain growth.

Let's get practical!   1

Search 'RCPCH centile charts' on the internet to see the centile charts for girls and boys aged 0 to 4.

What do you notice? How might these be helpful for parents and health professionals?

The checks that are carried out on the baby within one to five days of birth and the reasons why

A health professional, such as a doctor, nurse or midwife, will usually offer parents a more detailed physical examination of the baby within 72 hours. Although this examination is not compulsory, it is recommended as any problems found by the health professional can be treated quickly and the baby can be referred for further tests if needed. However, problems are rare. The results are given to the parents straight away and recorded in the baby's Personal Child Health Record (Red Book). The examination also gives health professionals the opportunity to talk to the new mother about how she is feeling and to identify any issues or concerns, for example with feeding.

Physical examination

Figure 1.31 shows the physical checks that are carried out on a new baby by a health professional and the reasons why.

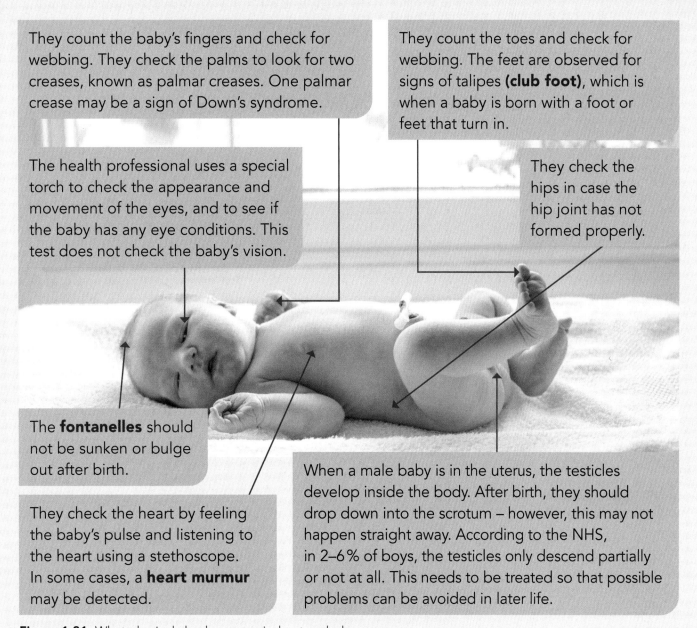

They count the baby's fingers and check for webbing. They check the palms to look for two creases, known as palmar creases. One palmar crease may be a sign of Down's syndrome.

They count the toes and check for webbing. The feet are observed for signs of talipes (**club foot**), which is when a baby is born with a foot or feet that turn in.

The health professional uses a special torch to check the appearance and movement of the eyes, and to see if the baby has any eye conditions. This test does not check the baby's vision.

They check the hips in case the hip joint has not formed properly.

The **fontanelles** should not be sunken or bulge out after birth.

When a male baby is in the uterus, the testicles develop inside the body. After birth, they should drop down into the scrotum – however, this may not happen straight away. According to the NHS, in 2–6% of boys, the testicles only descend partially or not at all. This needs to be treated so that possible problems can be avoided in later life.

They check the heart by feeling the baby's pulse and listening to the heart using a stethoscope. In some cases, a **heart murmur** may be detected.

Figure 1.31: What physical checks are carried out and why

Heel prick test

The heel prick test is a blood test which all babies are given when they are five days old. It tests for nine rare but serious health conditions. The more well-known of these are:

- sickle cell disease (an inherited blood disease)
- cystic fibrosis (an inherited condition which affects the lungs and the way food is digested)
- congenital hypothyroidism (a condition which affects babies' growth and can cause learning disabilities).

The remaining six are inherited metabolic diseases, which affect the metabolism. Although they all have different symptoms, those affected can become very seriously ill and they can be life threatening.

A baby is more likely to have one of these conditions if either of the parents has them. By testing at this early stage, the baby is able to have early treatment which can help to prevent severe disability or death.

Test your knowledge   1

1 Look at the following sentences and match them to 'vernix' or 'lanugo':

    a   Is a soft, fine hair covering

    b   Protects the baby from infections

    c   Keeps the skin moist

    d   Is a white waxy protective substance

    e   Keeps the baby's body at the right temperature

    f   Is absorbed into the skin after birth.

2 Are the following true or false?

    a   The heel prick test is a check for nine rare health conditions.

    b   An eye examination will check the baby's vision within five days of birth.

    c   The fontanelles should not be sunken or bulge out.

    d   A male baby's scrotum should be checked for testicles.

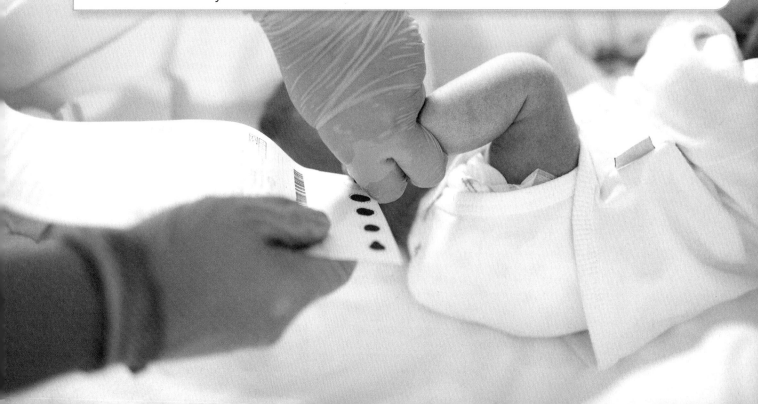

3.2 Postnatal care of the mother and baby

What kind of help might a new family need in the first few weeks?
How might they access this support?

Figure 1.32: Postnatal care

The role of the health visitor in supporting the new family

A health visitor is a registered nurse or midwife who has had additional training and qualifications. This enables them to work with families and individuals in the wider community. Health visitors are based in GP surgeries, community clinics or health centres. Their key focus is preschool children and their families, although they are primarily involved with the care and support of babies and new parents.

After a baby is born, the health visitor is the family's main source of advice and support. Health visitors provide a range of information and advice to families and liaise with other health professionals if needed.

They visit new parents before the birth of their baby, so that they can discuss what support might be needed and to answer any questions the parents may have. After this, they are likely to have several other scheduled visits although this depends on the needs of the family.

Visits usually take place:

*   before the birth, at around 28–32 weeks of pregnancy

*   when the baby is 10–14 days old

*   six to eight weeks after the birth

*   one year after the birth for a developmental review (a check on the baby's development)

*   two to two and a half years after the birth for a developmental review.

Health visitors also talk to parents about how their baby's health and development will be monitored in their Personal Child Health Record (Red Book), which they will give to them. The Red Book is a source of information and advice which can be helpful to new parents. It is also where immunisations and weight checks are recorded, as well as any details which the parents would like to add.

Figure 1.33 summarises the main aspects of a health visitor's role.

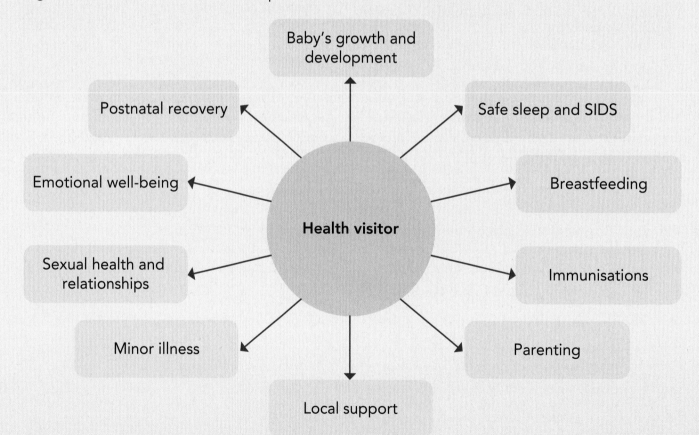

Figure 1.33: Aspects of a health visitor's role

Let's get practical! 2

Use a computer to create a leaflet informing new parents about the role of the health visitor and how they can help to support parents.

Safe sleeping – Sudden Infant Death Syndrome (SIDS) and how to reduce the risk

SIDS, or cot death, is the name given to the death of an apparently healthy baby within the first six months. According to the Lullaby Trust, SIDS affects around 230 babies a year in the UK, usually when they are asleep. The advice to reduce the risk is therefore around safe sleeping. Although it is not clear what causes SIDS, there are some steps which new parents can take to reduce the risk to their baby (see Table 1.15).

Table 1.15: The dos and don'ts to protect babies from SIDS

Do	Don't
• Place the baby on its back to sleep. • Put the baby in its cot, Moses basket or pram with its feet touching the end. • Make sure the baby's head is uncovered – the blanket should not be any higher than shoulder height. • Have the baby sleep in the same room as its parents for the first six months. • Make sure the baby's mattress is in a good condition. It should be firm, flat and waterproof. • Breastfeed where possible.	• The mother should not smoke during pregnancy. Do not allow smoking in the same room either before or after the baby is born. • Do not sleep with a baby on a bed or in a sofa or armchair. • Parents should not share a bed with their baby, particularly if either of them takes drugs, drinks alcohol or smokes. • Do not allow a baby to become too hot or too cold. Babies should be in a room of between 16 and 20 °C and have light bedding or a lightweight sleeping bag.

How partner, family and friends can provide physical and emotional support

In the first few weeks, the mother's partner, family and friends are an important source of help (see Figure 1.34). This may be on both a physical and emotional level.

Physical support may include helping out with practical tasks such as going shopping, cooking meals and general housework. Close friends and family who have experience in looking after a newborn may also be able to offer practical ideas and advice if they are needed.

New mothers are likely to need emotional support. Having a baby is an emotional experience for many reasons. This is partly because of the hormonal changes in the woman's body, as well as the rush of love which is felt by new parents and the pressure of new responsibilities. New mothers will be tired as they recover from giving birth and any surgery or medical procedures which they may have had during the process. This, combined with broken nights' sleep as they settle into feeding routines, is likely to mean that their emotions are heightened.

Figure 1.34: Physical and emotional support from family and friends is always beneficial to a new family.

The purpose of the mother's six-week postnatal check with the GP

The mother's six-week postnatal check usually takes place between six and eight weeks after the baby's birth. It usually follows on from the baby's six- to eight-week check although it can be done at a different time if needed. The postnatal check is carried out by a GP and is to make sure that the mother is recovering from giving birth and to check how she is feeling. She can also ask for this check earlier if she feels that it is needed.

The health checks may vary according to location but the check should include:

- asking the mother about her mental health and well-being following the baby's birth – this is to check whether she might have postnatal depression (a form of low mood and depression following the birth of a baby)

- talking to the mother about her physical health and whether she has had a period since the birth of her baby, or if she has had any vaginal discharge

- a physical examination to check the healing of any stitches following an **episiotomy** or caesarean section

- a blood pressure check if there have been any related problems during pregnancy or childbirth

- a weight check if the mother is overweight or obese to check her BMI

- a discussion about contraception

- scheduling cervical screening (a regular screening to check the health of the cervix) if this was due to take place during pregnancy.

The mother will also be given the opportunity to ask questions or discuss any concerns which she may have following the birth of her baby.

Over to you!　　2

For each of the types of support in the list below, decide whether they are given by a partner, a health visitor, family and friends or a GP. Some types of support may be given by more than one type of person.

- Advice on SIDS

- Emotional support

- Childcare experience

- Breastfeeding support

- Advice on contraception

- Advice on inoculation/vaccines

Continued

- Advice on the baby's growth and development
- Advice and support with feeding routines
- Physical support
- Help with postnatal depression
- Practical help
- Medical help following a caesarean section or episiotomy

3.3 The developmental needs of children from birth to five years

Let's get started   3

'Every child has the right to the best possible health, including healthcare, water and food, and a clean environment and education on health and wellbeing.'

United Nation's Convention on the Rights of the Child

What do you think children need in order to thrive (do well)?
Why is each one important?

Babies and young children rely on us, as adults, to meet their needs as they are unable to care for themselves independently. The way in which we are able to meet these needs has an impact on the child's development in different areas as well as their ability to meet their potential (see Figure 1.35).

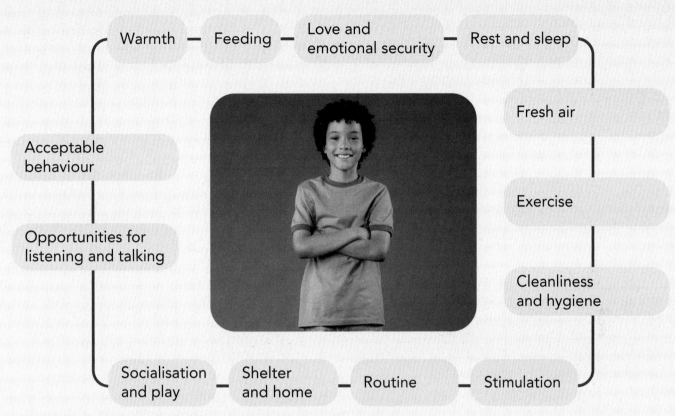

Warmth — Feeding — Love and emotional security — Rest and sleep

Acceptable behaviour

Opportunities for listening and talking

Fresh air

Exercise

Cleanliness and hygiene

Socialisation and play — Shelter and home — Routine — Stimulation

Figure 1.35: What children need to grow and develop successfully

Warmth

Always make sure that babies and young children are in an environment which is not too warm or too cold for any length of time, as extremes of temperature can have a harmful effect on their health and development. It is very important to check a baby's temperature as they are not able to tell you if they are too warm or too cold.

According to the Lullaby Trust, babies are at more risk of SIDS if they become too hot: a baby should ideally be in a room which is around 16–20 °C (65 °F). They should not wear hats or anything around their head when they are asleep indoors, as this may cause them to overheat.

When they are outside, always keep babies out of direct sun, as their skin has not yet developed enough pigment to protect them; you should apply sunscreen and shade them from the sun.

In cold environments, babies' bodies lose heat more quickly than they can produce it, and they do not have enough energy levels to keep themselves warm. You should use a thermometer to check the temperature in the room where the baby is sleeping, and a fan to keep the room cool in warmer weather. In babies and very young children, being too cold means their skin becomes red and cold to the touch. Babies and children should have the correct clothing to keep warm and their heads and feet should be covered in very cold weather so that they are insulated against the cold.

As children grow older, they are able to tell us if they are too warm or too cold, and you can tell them to drink more water if they are overheating or put more clothes on if they are cold. You can also teach them about the dangers of being too hot or too cold and why it is important to keep warm.

Over to you!   3

Imagine you are a health visitor and regularly visit different families as part of your role. One of the families you are working with has twin babies who are six months old. It is winter and particularly cold, and you are concerned that the babies are not warm enough.

a   Outline what you could say to the parents to explain why the babies need to be kept warm.

b   Describe the changes you could suggest to the parents to help them to make sure the babies are warm enough.

Feeding

In the first few months, new parents are likely to have advice from midwives about how to feed their baby, how much milk the baby needs and how to settle into a feeding pattern. Newborn babies do not need very much milk. According to the NHS they need around 150 to 200 ml per kilo of their weight each day depending on their needs. This gradually increases until they are ready to be **weaned** and start to eat **solids**, which usually takes place around the age of six months.

Knowing the correct type of food to give children is very important. Young children need a diet that includes the right vitamins and minerals as this is a period of rapid growth and development. You can ensure this by giving them a variety of foods from each of the different food groups as part of a **balanced diet**.

It's also important for children to eat the right amount of food. As children start to move on to solid food, you need to remember that they do not need as much food as adults, and their portions should be smaller. See R058, Topic Area 3, Section 3.1 for more information about nutrition.

Feeding routines and set mealtimes help to ensure that children develop healthy habits around eating and diet. Issues such as obesity, poor diet, eating disorders and **Type 2 diabetes** are a growing problem for the population in the UK, and many of these habits are set down in early childhood.

Over to you!   4

In your role as a health visitor, the twin family you are working with have asked for your help because the babies are finding it hard to settle after they have had a feed. They are six and a half months old and are being bottle-fed.

a   Describe the suggestions you could make to support the parents, justifying your reasons.

b   Outline how you could support the parents in a practical way.

Love and emotional security

The need for love and emotional security is present throughout life but it is particularly important for babies' and young children's emotional development. They need to feel that they are unconditionally loved and secure, and have a sense of belonging to their family as well as the wider community. This helps them to develop a sense of identity and of their place in the world.

At the earliest stages, babies develop key relationships or attachments, and different theorists (people who try to explain why things happen) have set out why these are important. Children's earliest attachments are usually to their parents but may also be with other key people in their lives. As they grow older, the quality of these attachments has a strong influence on how they form other relationships. For example, if a young child is brought up by a distant or abusive parent, they are likely to find it difficult to trust adults in general, will feel more insecure in close relationships and be more detached themselves. They may also be more withdrawn, or demonstrate attention-seeking behaviour. There are likely to be long-term effects for their emotional health and development. A child who grows up in a home in which they feel loved and protected because they have secure and loving attachments will find it easier to relate to others and form their own relationships.

Rest and sleep

Children need to have the right amount of rest and sleep for their physical health as well as their well-being and development. Children who are deprived of sleep may be affected in different ways, but it usually impacts on their mood and behaviour. This means that they may have regular tantrums or be more irritable and find it harder to control their emotions.

It is important that adults remember that children of different ages need different amounts of sleep (see Table 1.16).

Table 1.16: Amount of sleep needed by children 0–5 (Source: NHS)

Age of child	Approximate hours of sleep needed
4–12 months	12–16 hours including naps
1–2 years	11–14 hours including naps
3–5 years	10–13 hours including naps

Fresh air and exercise

Fresh air and exercise are very important for a young child's physical and mental health, as well as their development (see Figure 1.36). In order to develop physically, they need to have opportunities to be active and to move their whole body around. This helps with the development of their muscles and their physical health and fitness. (See R059, Topic Area 1, Section 1.1.) Being outside also stimulates the senses and gives children opportunities to explore the natural world and to take risks. This is an important part of building confidence and independence.

Many of us spend too much time indoors, particularly during the winter months. According to the World Health Organization, this is around 90 percent of our time. Being inside with poor air circulation can cause a range of health issues and lead to poorer concentration. Fresh air encourages children to move around and engage in play activities. Studies have shown that babies sleep better after spending some time outside during the day. Being outside gives us more opportunities to take in vitamin D and for children's lungs to develop and become stronger. The fresh air can also have a positive impact on mental health and mood. Adults need to act as role models and to show young children that being active outside can help them feel good as well as support their health and fitness.

Figure 1.36: How do fresh air and exercise help children's development?

Cleanliness and hygiene

Babies and young children are more vulnerable to illness and infection than adults as their immune systems are still developing, and so cleanliness and hygiene are very important.

Although babies do not need to be bathed every day, the area around the navel needs to be bathed carefully for the first week until remnants of the umbilical cord have gone, and the nappy area always needs to be kept clean to prevent soreness. Usually, the health visitor or midwife will show parents how to bathe a young baby and to ensure that the nappy area and skin creases are dried carefully. Babies who are fed with formula milk also need to be protected from **bacteria**, and this is done by thoroughly sterilising bottles and any other equipment which has been used. (See R058, Topic Area 3, Section 3.3.)

As children grow and develop, you need to continue to teach them about the importance of personal hygiene so that they develop good lifelong habits. One of the ways you can do this is by acting as a role model, as young children copy the adults around them. Keeping clean should be part of their routine and they should start to understand the relationship between this and the spread of germs. This should include handwashing, for example after using the toilet, before eating and after handling animals. They should also understand the importance of good oral hygiene and how diet influences the care of their teeth.

Let's get practical!   **3**

Create a poster for young children for display next to the basins in a nursery, showing them how to wash their hands carefully step by step. You can use illustrations or photographs.

Stimulation

As we learn more about the development of the brain, we understand more about the importance of stimulating babies in the early stages by interacting and communicating with them – touching and holding them, smiling and making faces at them, and encouraging them to respond. This affects language, intellectual, social and emotional development. Communicating with a baby in this way and giving them new experiences helps their brain to develop connections and pathways, which are very important as their brain is growing and changing very rapidly. As the child grows, the connections develop and strengthen as experiences and forms of communication are repeated.

Routine

Routines help to support a child's emotional development by making them feel safe. This is because they start to develop an awareness of 'what happens next'. When children do not know what is happening next on a regular basis they are likely to become anxious. Knowing about routines is also important for adults who are caring for children as they break up the day and ensure that children are getting appropriate care in different areas such as cleanliness and mealtimes.

Bath time

An example of a child's regular bedtime routine is knowing that after they have a bath and a story, it is bedtime. This familiarity and routine helps children to settle and go to sleep.

Over to you!   5

In your role as a health visitor, the twin family you are working with are having difficulties with the babies' sleep. Dad is a shift worker so comes home at different times but he wants to see them before they go to bed. However, after he has seen them and played with them they are finding it hard to settle.

a   Outline what you could say to the parents to help them to understand what the babies need and make suggestions to help them.

b   Use the information given in Over to you! 3, 4 and 5 about this family. Assess the family's current needs.

c   Following on from question b discuss whether they need to be referred for additional support.

Feeding

Feeding babies and young children should also be part of a routine, as this gives shape to their day and ensures they are fed regularly. It also helps to ensure that babies and children have the right amount of nutrition. (See also 'Feeding' earlier in this section.)

Shelter and home environment

As well as having love and emotional security, babies and young children need to be kept in an environment where they feel physically secure. This is a basic need – they need to be kept warm and dry and be in comfortable surroundings. Living in cold or damp conditions affects children's physical development. It may also cause them to feel anxious about their surroundings, which will have an adverse effect on their emotional development.

Socialisation and play

Opportunities for **socialisation** and play are a vital part of children's social and emotional development. This is because play helps children to develop their independence and explore their environment as well as learning to cooperate and take turns with others. Socialisation and play also develop their ability to relate to and form positive relationships with others and learn to understand that others also have needs. As they grow older, they start to form friendships as they discover that they have things in common with other people.

Play is also important for children's physical development, as when they run around they develop muscle and bone strength.

Opportunities for listening and talking

Babies and young children need plenty of opportunities to listen and talk to others in their first few years. If this happens, they usually start to say a few words around their first birthday and are fluent in their language by around the age of four. The development of language is important because as well as being a form of communication, it is linked to other key areas of a child's development. As with other areas, this is an important stage in a child's neural (brain) development and if a young child does not have language and communication opportunities, it will be harder for them to catch up later (see Table 1.17).

Table 1.17: How listening and talking help children's development

Area of development	Influence of listening and talking
Social development	Through listening and talking to others, children develop relationships and friendships with those around them. They learn about different social situations and start to understand empathy (the ability to understand the point of view or feelings of another person) and cooperation. This also affects their behaviour and how they relate to others.
Emotional needs	Being able to use language enables children to be able to express their feelings. Having adults who are role models (people whose good behaviour they admire and try to copy) and show them how to do this supports their ability to cope with different situations. This is important because a child who is unable to express their feelings is likely to become frustrated or to behave inappropriately.
Cognitive (intellectual) development	Through listening and talking, children develop the ability to use their memory. They start to be able to organise and express their thoughts, as well as to reason and develop their ideas when both speaking and writing. As they grow older, they have the ability to use more complex and abstract ideas, and a wider vocabulary gives them the tools to argue, solve problems and negotiate more effectively.

For more information see R059, Topic Area 1, Section 1.1.

Acceptable patterns of behaviour

Young children need to learn about acceptable patterns of behaviour as they start to mix with their peers and go out into the world. They need to develop an awareness and consideration for others and learn which types of behaviour are not socially acceptable and why. Very young children find this difficult as they are not mature enough to understand empathy or be able to reason why they should not use certain behaviour. They look to adults to give them clear and consistent boundaries and act as role models for how to treat other people.

They also need to learn that some types of behaviour can be dangerous. For example, when walking with an adult they need to know that they should hold hands and not run off close to a road. They start to learn about rules and why they need to follow them.

As children's language skills develop, you can start to talk to them about why certain behaviour is not acceptable and help them to be more considerate by talking things through with them. Give children plenty of positive praise when they are demonstrating the right kinds of behaviour. This gives them a feeling of approval so that they are more likely to repeat the behaviour.

Stretch

Lucy is four years old and will start school next month. She lives with her parents and her baby brother Zac in a small basement flat with a garden. There have been some signs of damp in the flat which is a concern with a new baby.

The family are close and regularly see both sets of grandparents but have very little money as Lucy's father has been made redundant from his job and her mother is still on maternity leave after having her baby brother. The landlord has threatened to evict them if they are unable to pay the rent for a third month running, although her maternal grandmother has said that they can stay with her if they need to. The family have been getting very little sleep as the baby does not yet sleep through the night.

Lucy knows some of her letters, is able to hold a pencil and can attempt to write her name. She can count to 12 and has several friends in preschool. She is well behaved for her age and enjoys books and playing with her friends, although lately her parents have noticed that she is quieter than usual.

Continued

1 Using the information above, evaluate whether Lucy's parents are currently able to meet her developmental needs and those of her brother.

2 Analyse some of the areas in which they may need to plan carefully so that the children's needs can be met and discuss how they might do this.

3 Discuss how Lucy's parents might develop an action plan with their health visitor to support both their children and the well-being of their family.

Case study

Raoul's story

Raoul is three years old and has an English mother and a French father who each speak to him all the time in their language. Although he was slow to start talking and did not speak very much before the age of 18 months, he now chats to both parents and speaks a number of words in each language; he can also count to ten in both languages.

Figure 1.37: Raoul

Raoul has a number of English cousins that he sees regularly, and he plays confidently and happily with them. His mother often drops him off at their house and he is happy to go without his parents staying with him. They often take him for days out and he is very interested in spiders and other insects.

Raoul enjoys playing on his tricycle and scooter and is able to run around and kick a ball confidently. He can put on his shoes and is almost able to do up his coat. Although his mother says that he can be a fussy eater, he usually sleeps very well. At his two-and-a-half-year developmental check, he had met all of the expected milestones for his age.

Check your understanding

1 Has speaking two languages affected Raoul's language development?

2 How have Raoul's parents given him opportunities for stimulation and development in different areas?

3 How many hours of sleep should Raoul have per night based on his age?

Review your learning

Test your knowledge   2

Copy and complete the following sentences, using the words below:

social   communication   meet   rely   physical   interaction   emotional   vulnerable

1   Babies and young children _____ on us to _____ their needs.

2   Rest and sleep are important for a child's _____ health.

3   Babies and young children are more _____ than adults to illness and infection.

4   Stimulation refers to _____ and _____ with children.

5   Socialisation and play are an important part of children's _____ and _____ development.

What have you learnt?

	See section
• Postnatal checks.	3.1
• Postnatal care of the mother and baby.	3.2
• The developmental needs of children from birth to five years.	3.3

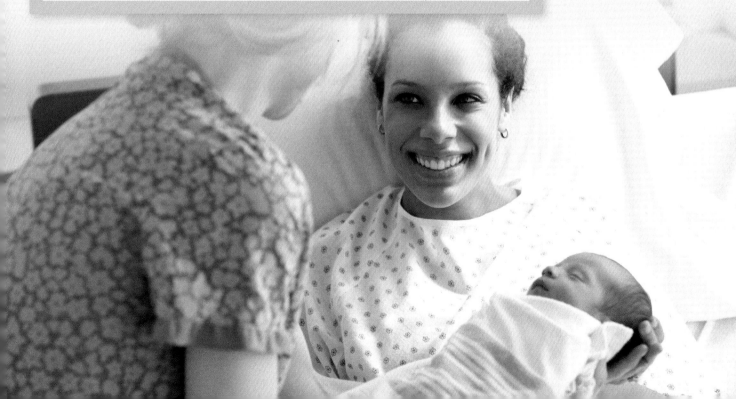

TA4

Childhood illnesses and a child-safe environment

Let's get started   1

How do you know what to do when you or someone around you is ill? Would this be any different in the case of a child?

Figure 1.38: Childhood illness

What will you learn?

- Recognise general signs and symptoms of illness in children.
- How to meet the needs of an ill child.
- How to ensure a child-friendly safe environment.

4.1 Recognise general signs and symptoms of illness in children

All those who work with babies and children need to be able to recognise some of the general signs and symptoms of illness (see Figure 1.39). This is because very young children are not able to say how they are feeling or may not even know that they are unwell.

Illnesses and infections are usually spread by close contact with someone who is infected. They may be breathed in or passed on by touching something which has bacteria or a virus on it. As young children regularly put their fingers in their mouths, this can happen easily.

You need to move a sick child away from others to prevent the infection spreading. You need to keep the child warm and comfortable and check on them regularly. Ask a first aider to look after them. Call their parent and ask them to come and collect the child. Do not give the child medication unless the parents have given written permission.

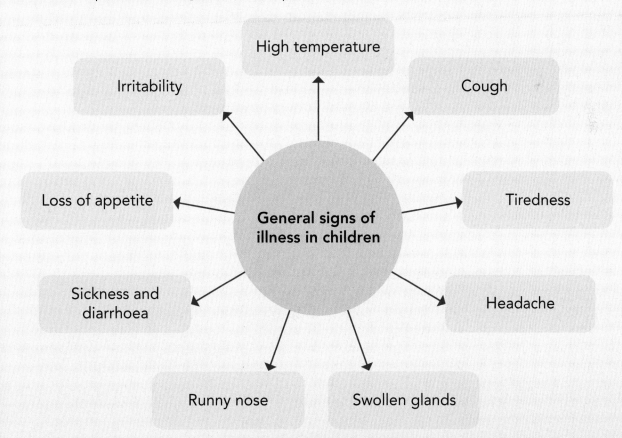

Figure 1.39: Children may have a range of symptoms if they are unwell.

Key signs, symptoms and treatment of illness in children

Mumps

Mumps will pass in one or two weeks. With appropriate permission, the caregiver might give the child painkillers such as junior paracetamol and they will need plenty of rest and fluids. Gently putting a warm compress or sponge pressed on their swollen glands may help ease the pain. They may need to eat soft foods and use a straw as chewing and swallowing can be difficult. Parents should keep a child with mumps at home. Mumps is highly **contagious** and is a **notifiable disease** (one which by law must be reported to the authorities) (see Figure 1.40).

Figure 1.40: This child is feeling poorly with mumps.

The signs and symptoms of mumps are:

- headache

- joint pain

- high temperature

- swollen, painful glands behind the ears.

Measles

Measles usually gets better within seven to ten days. There is no specific treatment for measles. With appropriate permission, the caregiver might give the child junior paracetamol to reduce their fever, and they will need plenty of rest and fluids. They may also prefer to stay in a darkened room. You can clean their eyes using cotton wool and water. Measles is highly infectious and is a notifiable disease (see Figure 1.41).

Figure 1.41: This child has measles.

The signs and symptoms of measles are:

- feeling generally unwell

- cold and high fever

- cough

- white or grey lesions (spot marks) inside and around mouth
- red rash which starts behind the ears and moves on to the face
- a swollen face
- sensitivity to light.

Meningitis

Meningitis can be fatal as it is an infection of the membranes which surround the brain and spinal cord. It can have long-term effects such as loss of hearing or vision. In some cases, a child with meningitis may get worse very quickly. While waiting for the ambulance to arrive, you should keep the child cool and reassure them. You should take them to hospital to be treated with antibiotics as soon as possible. Depending on the severity of the illness, the child may be treated at home afterwards with plenty of rest and fluids. Meningitis is a notifiable disease.

The signs and symptoms of meningitis are:

- high temperature
- seizures
- stiff neck
- aching head and muscles
- vomiting and drowsiness
- a red rash which does not fade under pressure
- dislike of bright lights
- listlessness (limpness) or a refusal to feed in babies.

Tonsillitis

There is no treatment for viral tonsillitis although with appropriate permission the caregiver might give the child painkillers to reduce the pain and their temperature. They will usually recover in three or four days. If the child has the less common bacterial tonsillitis, a GP may prescribe them antibiotics. In both cases they should rest, have plenty to drink and eat soft foods, as swallowing may be painful (see Figure 1.42).

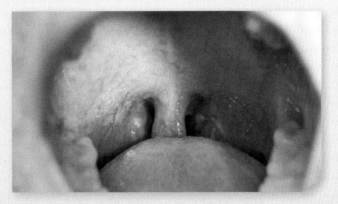

Figure 1.42: The tonsils are sore and swollen.

The signs and symptoms of tonsillitis are:

- sore throat and high temperature
- white spots on the tonsils
- headache/earache
- tiredness.

Chickenpox

There is no specific treatment for chickenpox, as it is usually a mild illness.

As the blisters are itchy, keep the child's fingernails short to prevent secondary infection. Put calamine lotion on the blisters to soothe them. The child should have plenty of rest and fluids, and, with appropriate permission, the caregiver might give them junior paracetamol to bring down any fever. If the blisters become infected, or the child has difficulty in breathing, a doctor should see them immediately. Chickenpox is highly contagious until the spots have become scabs. It is very common in children under ten.

The signs and symptoms of chickenpox are:

- red, itchy blisters on the trunk (body) and limbs
- temperature
- headache
- aching limbs.

Common cold

The common cold is a virus which spreads easily, particularly in young children who may be in close contact with each other. There is no specific treatment, but children should have plenty to drink. With appropriate permission, the caregiver might also give them junior paracetamol.

The signs and symptoms of a cold are:

- runny nose and sneezing
- sore throat or ears
- muscle aches
- possible temperature.

Gastroenteritis

If a child has gastroenteritis, it is important to replace lost fluids, so give them plenty of water or rehydrating solutions. Rehydrating solutions are available from chemists. Children should avoid drinking fizzy drinks or fruit juice as they can make the symptoms worse. They should rest and, with appropriate permission, can be given junior paracetamol if they have a fever. When they are ready to eat, give them plain food such as soup or bread.

You should seek urgent medical attention if they have been vomiting for three days or more, or have had diarrhoea for more than one week.

The signs and symptoms of gastroenteritis are:

- sickness and diarrhoea

- high temperature

- aches and pains.

Over to you! 1

You are working with a child and you notice he is not behaving as he normally does. He is not interested in playing with his friends and seems hot and flushed. He has a runny nose and a sore throat. You have called his mother who is unable to come and collect him for a couple of hours as she is at work some distance away.

Describe with reasons what you should do to help him while you are waiting for his mother to arrive.

Let's get practical! 1

Find out where medicines are kept in your setting. This may include inhalers and spacers for asthma, EpiPens for allergies, and junior paracetamol for coughs and colds. (An EpiPen is an adrenaline pump which is prescribed by a GP for children who have severe allergies.)

Find out the answers to these questions.

1 Who is responsible for giving medicine to children? Should they be trained in all cases?

2 What paperwork needs to be filled in when medicines are given?

3 How do you know which children have regular medication and whether they are able to take it themselves (for example, in the case of asthma inhalers)?

When to seek emergency medical help

In some cases, babies and children will need emergency medical help. This may happen because the signs and symptoms have worsened and you are concerned. If this happens, call an ambulance. If their parent is still some distance away, call them and ask them to meet you at the hospital.

In the case of infectious diseases, time is of great importance as a young child's immune system is still developing and it is harder for them to fight the infection. If you think a child needs urgent medical attention, call an ambulance straight away. If you are at all unsure, always seek help and dial 999 rather than waiting to see what happens. You should always know about and follow your setting's procedures for reporting accidents and emergencies.

Breathing difficulties

If the child is finding it hard to breathe, breathing fast or turning blue, you must seek emergency medical help immediately. Breathing difficulties which gradually worsen may be caused by an infection such as pneumonia or a chest infection; in this situation the child is also likely to have a temperature. If breathing difficulties are sudden or the child is choking, they may have a blocked airway.

Keep children who are having difficulties breathing in a comfortable upright position, leaning forward so that it is easier to breathe until help arrives.

Breathing difficulties can also be a sign of asthma. It is essential that you know which children in your setting have asthma as these attacks may be life threatening. They may have an inhaler to use during an asthma attack. These are usually kept in a place which is easily accessible to adults.

Unresponsive or limp

If a child is not moving and is drowsy or limp, or if you are unable to wake them up by shaking them by the shoulders, this means that they are unresponsive. You should call for an ambulance and put them on their side in the recovery position with their head tilted back to ensure that the airway is kept open until help arrives.

Let's get practical!   2

Find out how to put an adult or child into the recovery position.

Find out how to put a baby into the recovery position.

If it helps you to remember, carry out a practical session and practise on a friend or colleague.

High fever

Call an ambulance if a baby is under three months old and has a temperature of 38°C, or over 39°C if they are between three and six months old. Seek emergency medical attention if a child has a temperature of over 38°C that you are unable to bring down with junior paracetamol.

Seizures/fitting

Seek urgent medical attention by calling an ambulance on 999 if a child has a seizure or febrile convulsion (fit). The signs may be twitching of the muscles, an arched back and clenched fists. In some cases, the child may become unconscious. Keep the area around the child clear and place soft items around them. Once the seizure passes, put the child in the recovery position until help arrives.

Test your knowledge   1

Which of the following situations require emergency help?

a A baby under three months who has a high fever

b A young child who has a temperature and a rash which does not fade under pressure

c A child who has a notifiable disease

d A child who is limp or unresponsive

e A child who has chickenpox

4.2 How to meet the needs of an ill child

You need to know how to meet the different needs of a child who is ill so that you can care for them appropriately depending on their illness. You should think about the child's physical, intellectual, social and emotional needs. It may be that routines need to be changed, or that you have to sit and do activities with them so that they have some company. In all cases, you must keep the child comfortable and monitor them in case their condition changes.

Physical needs

In most cases, you need to keep a child who is unwell quiet and give them plenty of fluids. They are also likely to need lots of rest and sleep as their nights may be disturbed, particularly if they have a cough or have vomited. It is important to keep the child comfortable and to check on them regularly to ensure that their condition is stable.

Depending on the child's illness, they are likely to need some adjustments to their diet. For example, if they have gastroenteritis, they will need plenty to drink and some plain foods as their appetite returns. A child with mumps or tonsillitis may need to have softer food as swallowing is likely to be painful.

Children may need medication or painkillers during their illness so it is important to be aware of how often they should be taking it. If they are at the setting, you would need to ensure that you are authorised to give medication and be sure to follow any policies for administering it, for example keeping records and ensuring parents have given their permission.

You should be aware of children with any medical conditions as they may worsen as a result of illness. For example, asthma may be affected by a cough or cold. In cases of medical conditions such as epilepsy, the effectiveness of the epilepsy medication is likely to be affected if the child is vomiting as it will not be able to take effect, so you would need to be aware of this.

Social needs

Children who are unwell for any length of time are likely to miss social contacts. However, they may also be more easily upset by siblings or tire more quickly. If they are feeling better, they may benefit from games and visits with siblings or other family members if their infection is not contagious.

Emotional needs

Depending on their age and the illness, a young child who is unwell may be upset or confused, and is likely to need extra physical affection such as cuddles or extra time with an adult. It is possible that their behaviour may also regress, for example sucking their thumb. It may help to reassure them if they talk through any anxieties about the illness.

Intellectual needs

Young children may need some quiet activities to do for stimulation when they are unwell, particularly if they are in bed and unable to move around. They may enjoy colouring activities, books, watching television or the use of handheld devices to play games, although in cases where they are sensitive to light this may be painful for their eyes.

An older child who has a long-term illness or is spending extended time recovering may also need to have academic activities from school to support their continuing progress and development.

Case study

Sebastien

Sebastien is four, and has been absent from his Reception class for four weeks due to long-term illness: he is likely to be off school for another two weeks. His mother has been to see his teacher and has been given some educational activities to do at home. However, she has asked for some other suggestions as she says that he is very unhappy.

Check your understanding

1   Why might Sebastien be finding his recovery difficult?

2   Outline what suggestions could be made to support his needs.

3   Justify your suggestions.

4.3 How to ensure a child-friendly safe environment

Let's get started   3

Look at the picture. How many hazards can you see?

What can you do to ensure that the environment is safe for children?

Figure 1.43: Ensuring a child-friendly environment

What a hazard is

A **hazard** is something which could cause harm to others. This may mean a broken toy or a wet floor. Everyone should look out for hazards in the environment. We are all responsible for preventing hazards, so if you find something wrong you should always report it to those responsible and make it safe if you are able to. There are four different types of hazards:

- Physical hazards: these are items which are unsafe and may cause harm to the body, such as a piece of broken furniture, or something which is left on the floor which can be tripped over.

- Biological hazards: these are hazards which might impact on a person's health, such as viruses, bacteria, mould or bodily fluids. Animal excrement and vermin are biological hazards.

- Fire hazards: these might be items such as unsafe electrical appliances, or a large amount of waste materials or flammable liquids which have been stored together.

- Security hazards: these are doors and windows which have been left open, a hole in a fence, or a broken lock, which might pose a **risk**.

Recognise common hazards and how these can be prevented

According to RoSPA (the Royal Society for the Prevention of Accidents), there are more than 6000 deaths each year as a result of accidents within the home; children under five are among the most likely victims. This is because their lack of experience means they cannot predict the possible consequences of what they are doing. Different types of safety equipment are available and these should be used where possible as they can prevent harm from taking place.

Within the home

The types of hazards a child may be exposed to depend on the area in the home, and whether safety equipment is used. Homes where young children live or visit regularly will benefit from regular checks to ensure that hazards are kept to a minimum. In all cases, adults need to be vigilant to ensure that the environment is as safe as possible.

Keep young children out of the kitchen by using a stairgate in the doorway. In the kitchen, children are at risk from:

- **Scalds from hot water or steam:** use cordless kettles or those with a coiled flex. Never hold a child and a hot drink at the same time.

- **Burns from hot appliances:** use the rear hotplates/burners on a cooker hob and turn pan handles inwards. Use cooker guards so children can't reach up and pull on a pan handle.

- **Flames:** keep flammable objects such as tea towels away from the hob. Keep a fire blanket or fire extinguisher close by to prevent further damage in case of a fire. A smoke alarm will detect smoke and set off an alarm.

- **Cuts from knives, or broken glass or crockery:** store knives out of reach. Remove the child from the area if there are any breakages.

- **Cuts from glass window or doors:** make sure they are fitted with safety glass.

- **Poisoning from cleaning materials:** keep cleaning materials and household products out of reach or in a cupboard with childproof locks. Make sure hazardous products have child-resistant lids.

- **Slips and falls:** clean up any spillages from the floor straight away. Use childproof locks on windows.

- **Food poisoning and food safety hazards:** always keep sinks, fridges and surfaces where food is being prepared clean and change cleaning cloths and towels regularly. Use child-resistant containers to store food such as nuts. Use childproof locks on fridges and cupboards.

- **Choking on hard foods or round foods:** always cut up food items such as grapes and cherry tomatoes for younger children to prevent choking. Keep nuts away from small children.

In the toilet and bathroom, children are at risk from:

- **Scalds from hot bathwater:** fill the bath with cold water first and always test the water before letting a child get in the bath. Set the water thermostat at a lower temperature.

- **Drowning:** never leave young children alone in the bathroom. Always supervise children in the bath; they can drown in less than 3 cm of water.

- **Poisoning from cleaning materials:** keep cleaning materials and household products out of reach or in a cupboard with childproof locks.

- **Slips and falls:** clean up any spillages or splashes on the floor straight away.

- **Suffocation and choking:** keep nappy sacks out of children's reach. Make sure any blind cords are out of reach.

On the stairs, children are at risk from:

- **Falls:** use a stairgate at the top and bottom of the stairs. Fix faulty handrails straight away. Ensure stairways are well lit.

- **Trips and slips:** do not leave items on the stairs which could be tripped over. Fix carpets firmly.

It is important to always be vigilant when visiting outdoor spaces. In play areas/gardens, children are at risk from:

- **Drowning:** always supervise children in paddling pools and near ponds.

- **Poisoning from plants or berries:** check the garden for any plants with leaves or berries which could harm children.

- **Insecure shed or garage:** check that a shed or garage is locked and any unsafe equipment or chemicals have been put out of reach.

- **Animal faeces:** check the garden for faeces before letting children play outside.

- **Broken gates/holes in fencing:** ensure gardens are secure and children are unable to get out and access roads.

- **Play equipment:** check that any play equipment is safe.

Let's get practical!   3

Choose an area in a house or garden to carry out a 'health and safety walk'.

Look out for the common hazards which have been outlined above and evaluate whether any measures need to be taken to make the environment safe for a child.

Let's get practical!   4

Choose a room in a house. Design a poster to show potential hazards which new parents need to be cautious about, particularly when their baby starts walking.

Roads

You should always supervise young children when they are close to or crossing roads. They should be on safety reins, in a buggy or holding the hand of an adult. It is important for adults to talk to children about why they need to be cautious near roads and to set a good example, for example using pedestrian crossings where possible and crossing safely. This will help children to develop their own awareness of road hazards.

The Green Cross Code was created in 1970 as a six-step guide to raise awareness of road safety and to help children to remember the safest way to cross a road. By talking to children about these safe steps when you cross the road with them, you can help them learn how to cross the road safely.

Green Cross Code

1   **THINK!** Find the safest place to cross.

2   **STOP!** Stand on the pavement near the kerb.

3   **USE YOUR EYES AND EARS!** Look all around for traffic and listen.

4   **WAIT UNTIL IT IS SAFE TO CROSS!** If traffic is coming, let it pass. Then look all around again.

5   **LOOK AND LISTEN!** When it is safe, walk straight across the road – do not run.

6   **ARRIVE ALIVE!** Keep looking and listening while you cross.

Figure 1.44: Green Cross Code

Travelling in cars also presents a hazard, and children should always be fully restrained in appropriate car seats.

The importance of safety labelling

Safety labelling is used on different items such as toys, equipment or clothing in the UK, to identify that they are safe for use. Some of these are specific to babies and children, while others are for general use and may be found on a range of products (see Table 1.18).

Table 1.18: Different types of products may have a range of safety labels.

Label	Meaning and why it is used on specific products
BSI Kitemark	The BSI Kitemark is a quality mark that shows a product meets the applicable and appropriate British, European and other recognised international standards for quality, safety, performance and trust. Products which display the BSI Kitemark include bike helmets and safety glass.
Lion Mark	The Lion Mark was developed by the British Toy and Hobby Association (BTHA) which supplies around 90% of toys sold in the UK. It was developed in 1988 to act as a recognisable consumer symbol denoting safety and quality. Products which display the Lion Mark include soft toys.
Age Warning symbol	The Age Warning symbol is used to identify products which are not suitable for use by children under the age of three years. This is usually because they have small parts which are a choking hazard or cords that could cause strangulation. Products which display the Age Warning symbol include those which have small parts as these are a choking hazard for small children.
CE and UKCA symbols	The CE symbol is a European directive and by law must be displayed on many products which are for sale in the EU. This means that the product has been tested and is safe for use by children under 14 in line with the directive. It was used in the UK until January 2021 but has now been replaced by the UKCA mark, as the UK has left the EU. Products which display the CE and UKCA symbols include toys and educational products such as maths and sports equipment.
Children's nightwear labelling	Fabrics used for children's nightwear must comply with flammability performance requirements under the Nightwear (Safety) Regulations 1985. Compulsory labelling is in place to show that children's nightwear complies with these regulations. Some items, such as dressing gowns and bathrobes, are exempt from these requirements. However, if they do not conform to the Regulations, they must display labelling to indicate this. Products which display·this include nightdresses and pyjamas for children under the age of 13.
Children's dressing-up clothes	At time of writing, there is a review taking place of the fire safety of children's dressing up clothes, supported by RoSPA. In the meantime, there are two voluntary codes of practice for labelling to enhance their safety.

Review your learning

Test your knowledge   2

Identify the safety label from the definition:

1   Used on toys to symbolise toy safety and quality.

2   Used to show a product has been tested and is safe for use by children under 14.

3   A quality mark that shows a product has met British, European and recognised international standards for quality, safety, performance and trust.

4   Used to identify products which are not suitable for use by children under the age of three years.

What have you learnt?

	See section
• Recognise general signs and symptoms of illness in children.	4.1
• How to meet the needs of an ill child.	4.2
• How to ensure a child-friendly safe environment.	4.3

R058

Create a safe environment and understand the nutritional needs of children from birth to five years

Let's get started

Accidents happen! How do we keep children safe? How can we help children to be healthy?

What will you learn in this unit?

Babies and young children need a secure and nurturing environment in order to thrive (to grow and develop well). Measures must be in place to prevent harm, the equipment must be safe and suitable, and healthy meals should be offered.

In this unit you will learn about:

- creating a safe environment in a childcare setting **TA1**
- choosing suitable equipment for a childcare setting **TA2**
- nutritional needs of children from birth to five years **TA3**.

How you will be assessed

This unit will be assessed through a series of coursework tasks that show your understanding of each topic area. You will complete the assignment independently in class with teacher supervision. The assignment will be marked by your teacher. The assignment contains four tasks, which will cover:

- designing a plan of a safe environment in a day nursery
- choosing equipment in a day nursery
- recommending healthy meal choices in a day nursery.

Your teacher will also observe you preparing a feed or meal.

Creating a safe environment in a childcare setting

Let's get started

Look at the photos below. What might happen next?

Figure 2.1: Creating a safe environment in a childcare setting

What will you learn?

- Plan to create a safe environment in a childcare setting.

1.1 Plan to create a safe environment in a childcare setting

Reasons why accidents happen in a childcare setting

Figure 2.2 shows some reasons why **accidents** can happen.
Can you remember an accident you had as a child?
Can you link it to one (or more) of the reasons shown?

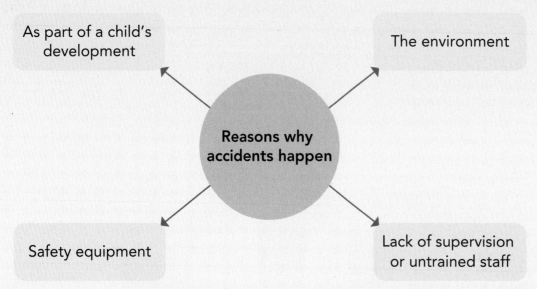

Figure 2.2: Reasons why accidents happen

The environment

A safe environment is important in order to prevent accidents. Children can be cared for in a range of settings, for example a day nursery, childminder, toddler group, playgroup or creche. Some children go to a forest school, which is set outside.

Let's get practical! 1

Go on a 'health and safety walk' around the room you are in. How many objects can you find that might be a choking **hazard** to small children?

Think about a childcare setting you are familiar with and the different areas within it. Let's look at the potential accidents waiting to happen in each areas.

In the feeding and dining area, children are at **risk** from:

- choking on hard foods, like whole nuts or boiled sweets, or round foods, like whole grapes, popcorn or cherry tomatoes

- suffocating if they put a plastic bag over their head or being strangled by a drawstring bag

- burns from hot appliances, such as heaters or ovens, or from matches, lighters and anything with a naked flame

- scalds from hot liquids such as a baby's milk feed, hot water from a tap or a staff member's cup of tea

- falls from highchairs

- electric shocks from faulty switches on equipment, from old or damaged appliances, or from water and electricity mixing

- poisoning from cleaning products, for example washing-up liquid, antibacterial spray

- food poisoning from contaminated food that has high levels of bacteria

- poisoning from medication belonging to staff or other children (see Figure 2.3) – taking medication that hasn't been prescribed to you personally can be dangerous; taking too much medication is also harmful.

Figure 2.3: Children might mistake pills for sweets. Child-resistant lids will not stop a determined child from opening a bottle of pills

- cuts from sharp objects such as knives, scissors or broken glass

- trapping their fingers in cupboards or drawers, or in the harness of their highchair

In the sleeping area, consider the risks from:

- babies being accidentally smothered by pillows or duvets when they are sleeping. Babies do not have strong neck muscles. It's possible for a baby to get stuck in a position where they are unable to breathe and not able to move their head

- babies being smothered or strangled by cot bumpers

- older babies climbing out of cots and falling

- toddlers wrapping unsecured blind cords around their necks or getting caught in them – they won't be able to remove a cord if it gets wrapped around their neck and it could strangle them

- older babies trapping their fingers in drop side cots.

In the changing and bathroom area:

- A child can suffer a chemical burn if they come into contact with chemicals, such as those found in cleaning fluids.

- Babies could roll off changing tables.

- Children could be poisoned by eating or drinking cleaning products, for example toilet cleaner, laundry capsules.

In the play and activity area, children are at risk from:

- choking by putting small objects in their mouth, such as small toy parts, buttons, coins, button batteries, marbles and pen tops

- being strangled by scarves in the dressing-up box

- burns from button batteries in toys; these can burn a hole in a child's throat and cause internal bleeding if swallowed (see Figure 2.4)

- falling after climbing up onto furniture – heavy furniture or equipment can cause serious **harm** if it falls onto a child; they might also climb upstairs and fall

- slipping on spills, tripping on objects such as toys, or tripping over trailing wires or loose carpets

- cuts from bumping their heads on the sharp corners of furniture

- trapping their fingers in doors and windows

- electric shocks from old or faulty plug sockets, or from loose wiring and poorly fitting sockets.

Figure 2.4: Why can the button batteries found in toys be a hazard to small children?

Let's get practical!   2

Have you ever stopped to think how many times a day you use electricity? You might switch on a light, turn on your TV or charge your phone. Electricity is needed in childcare settings too and with this comes the risk of electric shock.

Look around the room and see how many items require electricity. Are any of these found in childcare settings?

Accidents can happen in settings where children of different ages play together. A childminder must make sure that babies do not have access to toys that could harm them; some toys are only suitable for older children. In a creche, you need to check that the equipment is safe for all the children present.

When outside:

- Too much time in the sun can lead to sunburn, skin damage and eye damage.

- A child could be strangled by a skipping rope.

- Toddlers and older children are at risk of falling off climbing equipment.

- Babies and children can drown in paddling pools, ponds, water play tables, collected rainwater.

- Children could eat poisonous berries or plants, or be poisoned by drinking weed killer or other pest control products.

- Prickly plants, such as holly or thorns, can scratch a child's skin.

- Grazes can happen if a child falls on a hard surface, like the playground.

- Children could trap their fingers in reins or hinged play equipment.

Lack of supervision or untrained staff

Accidents can happen if there is a lack of supervision. For example:

- A baby who is learning to stand might pull themselves up onto furniture and then topple over.

- A toddler might put play dough in their mouth.

- A preschool child might play with the water when washing their hands and make the floor wet and slippery.

You will look at safe supervision in more detail later in this topic area.

If the staff caring for children are inexperienced or have not been professionally trained, they might not know enough about health and safety. This may mean that accidents are more likely to happen.

All childcare settings have a set of policies and procedures about caring for children and it is your responsibility to follow them. Specialist training providers offer courses on topics such as risk assessment, fire safety and accident prevention. Nannies and childminders, who often work alone with children, must be trained in paediatric first aid.

Safety equipment

Accidents can happen if:

- there is a lack of safety equipment
- safety equipment is not used correctly
- safety equipment is faulty or damaged
- safety equipment is not checked regularly for defects (faults).

As part of a child's development

You might have heard a parent say, 'Gosh, you're into everything!' as their small child touches everything in sight. It is perfectly natural for babies and children to be curious and want to explore their surroundings as they start to roll over, crawl, cruise, walk and then run. Minor bumps and grazes are commonplace as babies and toddlers become more mobile and practise new skills.

Babies and young children put things in their mouths and touch objects without understanding potential dangers. They aren't aware that they might trap their fingers if they swing on a cupboard door or that the bottle they are trying to open is full of a chemical that could make them ill.

Children watch and copy adults. If a child sees you cutting up fruit at snack time, they might want to have a go. They don't know that sharp knives can hurt them or how to use them safely.

It is your responsibility to prevent accidents in a childcare setting as much as you possibly can. As children get older, you can help them to understand the need for safety when tackling new challenges. This helps them start to learn how to manage risks for themselves. You will look at how to prevent accidents by educating the children later in this topic area.

Types of childhood accidents

Let's think about different types of childhood accidents. Look at Table 2.1.

Table 2.1: Types of childhood accidents

Accident	Explanation
Choking and suffocation	Choking is when an object blocks your airway and stops you from breathing.
	Babies and young children often put things in their mouth as part of how they explore the world around them. A child's airway is very narrow so it can easily be blocked by small objects.
	If your nose and mouth are covered and you cannot breathe, you will suffocate. This is because the oxygen supply to your lungs has been cut off. A child will suffocate more quickly than an adult; it can happen in just a few minutes.
	You can also suffocate if your throat is pressed or made narrower and you cannot breathe. This is called strangulation. A child could be strangled by getting a cord for a blind caught around their neck.
Burns	Burns are caused when your skin touches a very hot surface, for example an iron or a kettle.
	A scald is a type of burn caused by boiling water or steam.
	If swallowed, household products like drain cleaner or bleach can cause chemical burns internally (inside your body).
	Even a small burn can be very painful. Babies and children have thinner, more sensitive skin than an adult.
Falls	A fall is when you drop down onto the ground. Falls include falling over on one level and falling from a height.
	Trips and falls can cause minor bumps and bruises; children often trip over their own feet! Falling from a height can cause serious injury.
Electric shocks	An electric shock is when an electric current passes through your body. This can cause burns and damage to your organs, such as your heart or brain.
Drowning	Drowning happens when you are underwater and cannot breathe. Drowning can happen very quickly. Babies and children can drown in just a few centimetres of water.
Poisoning	Poisoning happens when you swallow or breathe in something dangerous that makes you ill. Poisoning is one of the most common reasons that children under five are taken to hospital.
Cuts and grazes	A cut is a wound caused by something sharp, like a knife or piece of broken glass. These wounds can be very serious.
	A graze is when the surface of your skin is scraped off or broken.
Trapped fingers	Trapping your fingers means getting them caught in something. This can cause bruising, swelling and even broken bones.

Let's get practical!   3

Choose one or more types of accident from Table 2.1. Use the internet to research how many times a year this type of accident happens to children under five in the UK.

Over to you!   1

Match the types of accidents to items that are found in childcare settings.

1   drowning   a   nappy sacks

2   poisoning   b   mop and bucket

3   burns   c   medication

4   falls   d   radiator

5   suffocation   e   highchair

Over to you!   2

1   This baby has learnt to pull himself up.
    He's having fun exploring! For each statement,
    name the type of accident that could happen.

    a   The baby might slam the drawer shut.

    b   The baby might climb up onto the drawer.

    c   There might be small objects in the drawer.

    d   The corner of the drawer might be sharp.

    e   There might be medication in the drawer.

2   Describe one more type of accident that could
    happen in this situation.

Figure 2.5: Babies like to explore.

Plan to prevent accidents in a childcare setting

It is very important to learn about ways of reducing the risk of injuries.
Think back to Unit R057, Section 4.3. What did you learn about creating a
child-friendly and safe environment?

Different areas in a childcare setting

Earlier in this unit you looked at the reasons why accidents happen in
different areas of a childcare setting. Figure 2.6 shows the areas you
might find.

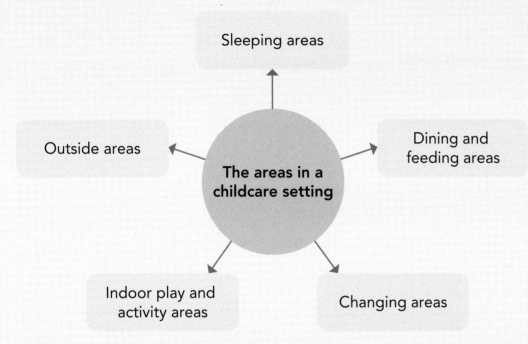

Figure 2.6: The areas in a childcare setting

From an early age, you can start to teach children about staying safe. By educating the children, you give them the tools to explore each area of the setting safely. For example:

- Use simple words or signs like 'hot' or 'sharp' with babies.

- Encourage walking rather than running inside.

- Teach children safety rules, for example, 'Do not climb on furniture' and 'Do not touch sharp knives'.

- Model how to use children's scissors and other tools safely.

- Include safety posters or photos in the environment, for example 'Only four children on the climbing frame'.

- Explain to older children why we follow safety rules. Talk about why only four children are allowed on the climbing frame at any one time, why we do not eat berries in the garden or why we never touch an oven.

Over to you!   3

During sand play, a child gets excited and starts throwing sand. A lot of sand ends up on the floor and it gets quite slippery.

What would you do? Choose two answers.

A   Put the lid on the sand box and tell the children the activity is over as they are being too silly.

B   Remind the children not to throw sand as it might hurt their friends and explain that the sand might make the floor slippery.

C   Sweep up the sand straight away to prevent any children or staff from slipping over.

D   Go and find a member of staff to tell, leaving the children unsupervised at the sand box.

Appropriate equipment for the area

The equipment in each area of the setting must be suitable and safe for the children to use.

- All equipment must conform to British Safety Standards – check the safety labels.

- Furniture should be child-sized; low-level tables and chairs help small children to sit safely when eating or taking part in tabletop activities.

- Only use furniture that is sturdy and stable. Make sure moveable furniture is safe and cannot tip over.

- Avoid furniture with sharp corners or edges.

- Make sure play resources are suitable for the ages and abilities of the children. Remember to check the manufacturers' recommendations.

When used correctly, safety equipment can help to prevent accidents. You can find more information about appropriate safety equipment in Unit R057, Topic Area 4, Section 4.3.

Placement of equipment in the area

Furniture needs to be arranged in a safe way. For example, in the sleep room it would not be sensible to place a cot under a shelf; a baby might reach up and pull items down on themselves. Imagine what might happen if chairs were placed in front of a safety gate; a child might use the chair to climb up and over the gate.

Equipment and resources must be stored or stacked safely to prevent them falling onto children. Equipment that could cause harm, such as electrical items, must be placed out of reach. Look at Figure 2.7.

When childcare settings are initially designed, the placement of fixed items such as sockets and outside taps must be considered to ensure safety.

Figure 2.7: A childminder may care for children of different ages together. How can furniture and play equipment be organised safely?

Supervision/staffing requirements for the area

Children must always be supervised to keep them safe. This means you must be constantly alert, both watching and listening. Some activities will require you to be extra vigilant. For example:

- Feeding areas: always supervise children at mealtimes and encourage them to sit down while eating and drinking.

- Play areas: some activities have an element of risk, for example cutting with scissors, woodwork or cookery. Others may use small items, such small pegs, sequins, role-play money or counters.

- Outside areas: make sure you can see all areas of the outdoor space where children are playing. Watch and be ready to support children using climbing or balancing apparatus. Challenging equipment can be fenced off to stop younger children using it, or if it is too slippery to use safely on a wet day (see Figure 2.8).

- Outings: all settings must meet the adult-to-child ratios required to keep children safe. On outings, more adults than usual will be needed to make sure children are fully supervised.

Figure 2.8: This toddler is getting more confident at climbing. How is this childcare setting helping to keep her safe?

Case study

Nursery school court case

In 2012, a little girl, aged three, died on her first day at nursery. During outside play, her neck became tangled in a rope while playing on the slide.

She was taken to hospital but tragically died.

At the court hearing, several failures were found that led to the child's death:

- She had been left unsupervised. The nursery's CCTV footage showed it was 20 minutes before a member of staff went to look for her.

- The location of the slide meant it was not visible to staff from the playground.

- There was no barrier around the slide to stop children going on unsupervised. This concern had previously been raised by staff members, but no action had been taken.

- The setting's risk assessment had identified that the rope could cause strangulation and that it should be put away when not in use. This hadn't happened.

The setting was fined £175 000.

Check your understanding

1   Identify three factors which led to this accident.

2   Describe what could have been done to prevent this from happening.

3   Explain how this case shows the need for constant supervision of young children.

Safety considerations

When you start training or working in a childcare setting, you will learn to be aware of potential hazards and how to keep children safe. All staff and volunteers in a childcare setting must be given training to help them work safely. It is a legal requirement that your induction training includes information about health and safety issues. You must receive food hygiene training if you are handling the children's food. You will also learn how to follow **risk assessments**.

A risk assessment is used to check that a childcare setting is safe (see Figure 2.9). It lists the potential hazards in the setting, so that measures can be put in place to lessen the risk of accidents and harm.

Risk Assessment Form			
Date of Risk Assessment: _____ Risk Assessment carried out by: _____			
Item/place/ activity/ outing to be assessed	Potential risk	Precautions in place	Person responsible for ensuring action is taken
Cots and highchairs	Injuries to children: Falls Cuts Bruises Trapped fingers Strangulation	All furniture is labelled with the CE symbol. All staff are trained on the safe use of furniture during their induction. Highchairs are fitted with five-point harnesses; these are always used. Cot sides are always raised while occupied to stop children falling out. All furniture is checked before use and removed if faulty. Furniture is stacked/stored safely away from children when not in use. Children are constantly monitored and supervised. Children only use furniture appropriate for their age group/abilities.	

Figure 2.9: A basic risk assessment of the furniture in a day nursery

> **Let's get practical!   4**
>
> 1 Outdoor play areas should always be checked before children use them to help prevent accidents. Go to your local play park and see if you can spot any of these hazards:
>
> • unwanted objects thrown or blown over the fence, for example litter, glass bottles, cans, syringes, cigarettes, plastic bags
>
> • broken fences or gates
>
> • gates left open
>
> • broken or damaged play equipment or surfaces
>
> • wet or slippery play equipment or surfaces
>
> • poisonous or prickly plants, for example stinging nettles
>
> • animal faeces on the grass, in the soil or in uncovered sand boxes
>
> • rainwater in pots or containers.
>
> 2 What other hazards did you notice?
>
> 3 Describe three ways to prevent accidents in the park.

Let's look at some safety considerations to prevent accidents in Table 2.2.

Table 2.2: Safety considerations

Types of accidents	Safety considerations
Choking	Do not give babies or toddlers hard food.
	Cut food for babies and toddlers into small pieces. Cut soft fruit such as grapes and blackberries into quarters. Raw vegetables and fruit should be cut into small strips, rather than rounds.
	Never leave a baby alone to feed with a propped-up bottle as they may choke on the milk.
	Keep small objects away from babies and toddlers. Keep toys designed for older children out of babies' and toddlers' reach.
	Do not use raw jelly cubes for messy play.
Suffocation	Use blankets (rather than duvets) with babies under one.
	Do not put pillows, cot bumpers or large soft toys in cots.
	Never place babies on beanbags to sleep.
	Keep plastic bags, such as shopping bags and nappy sacks, out of reach.
	Take care if carrying a baby in a baby sling; make sure they are not smothered.
	Remove anything that a child could wrap around their neck.
	Check curtain and blind cords are secured and out of reach.
	Do not tie dummies (also called pacifiers or soothers) to clothes using ribbons or cords.

Table 2.2: Continued

Types of accidents	Safety considerations
Burns	Test the temperature of formula milk before giving a bottle; be careful if serving hot food at mealtimes.
	Keep children away from ovens, kettles, hobs, radiators and heaters. Use safety equipment such as oven guards, fire guards and radiator covers.
	Check that low-level hot pipes are covered with insulating material.
	Use a thermostat to control the hot water temperature.
	Keep matches and lighters out of the reach and sight of children.
	Keep substances that can cause chemical burns (such as liquid laundry capsules and button batteries) out of the reach of children.
	Follow sun safety guidelines: apply sunscreen to babies and children, make sure they wear sun hats, make sure they stay in the shade when it is hot in the middle of the day.
	Keep hot drinks out of the reach of children. A hot drink can scald a child's skin even 15 minutes after it has been made.
Drowning	Supervise children when they are playing in or near water, or when they are in the bath.
	Ponds must be fenced off or covered.
	Empty out paddling pools and water trays straight after use.
	Check for and empty out any rainwater that has gathered in things like buckets or wheelbarrows outside.
Falls	Do not leave babies alone on changing tables as they could roll off; always keep one hand on them.
	Put cradles or bouncy chairs on the floor, not up on tables or beds.
	Use a five-point harness on highchairs and buggies to keep children secure.
	Do not put soft toys in cots as a more mobile baby can climb up onto the toys and fall out.
	Babies who are learning to walk may cruise around the room and hold onto furniture. All furniture must be stable so it doesn't topple onto them.
	Teach older children not to climb up onto furniture as they may fall.
	If there are stairs in the setting, use safety gates and keep the steps clear from things that people might trip over.
	Check the floor for items that could be tripped over, picking up toys as you go.
	Clean up spills, such as water or sand, straight away.
Electric shocks	Ideally, plug sockets should be out of children's reach. If this isn't possible, socket protector covers (which go around the plug and plug socket) should be used.
	Keep electrical equipment out of children's reach.
	Electrical equipment must be tested for safety every year by a qualified electrician. Faulty items must be removed straight away.
Poisoning	Keep medicine, cleaning products and any other toxic substances in a locked cupboard, out of children's reach and sight. Do not rely on child-resistant lids.
	Make sure art and craft resources, such as paint and glue, are suitable for children.
	Check if any plants inside the setting or outdoors are poisonous and if so, remove them.

Table 2.2: Continued

Types of accidents	Safety considerations
Cuts and grazes	Make sure doors, windows and any glass furniture at the children's level are made of safety glass. It will display the British Standards Institution (BSI) Kitemark (see R057, Topic Area 4, Section 4.3).
	Wrap any broken glass in newspaper and throw it in the bin straight away.
	Do not let babies or toddlers hold anything made of glass.
	Keep sharp objects out of children's reach. If you have been using scissors or knives, put them away straight after use.
	If older children are using safety scissors or child-friendly knives as part of an activity, you must supervise them carefully.
	Check inside the setting and the garden and remove any thorny or prickly plants.
	Some settings have safety surfaces outside to limit injuries if children fall. If this isn't available, place outdoor toys on grass or use rubber mats.
Trapped fingers	Use safety equipment, such as door catches or locks.
	Fit rubber strips to door hinges.
	Take care not to trap children's fingers or pinch their skin in the harness when strapping them into highchairs and buggies.
	Check toys and resources, such as toy boxes with hinged lids and folding equipment, for suitability.

Let's get practical!   5

The most common cause of choking in children is food. Babies and children can choke on small items of food such as grapes.

a   Practise cutting grapes into quarters lengthways, as if you were preparing them for a child.

b   Design a factsheet explaining how choking can happen and how it can be prevented.

Over to you!   4

State a piece of safety equipment that would prevent each of the accidents listed below:

a   Child trapping their fingers in a door.

b   Toddler falling down the stairs.

c   Baby touching a heater.

d   Child opening and falling out of a window.

e   Toddler bumping their head on the corner of a cabinet.

Reasons for plan choices

Planning a safe environment helps to prevent accidents in childcare settings. You have learnt about the importance of:

- staff training

- supervision

- having appropriate safety equipment

- sensible placement of equipment

- educating the children

- completing risk assessments.

Think about all these factors when planning each area of the setting.

Let's get practical!   6

Choose an area of a childcare setting and make a plan to show how accidents are prevented. You could cut pictures of furniture and resources from catalogues or draw your design. Label your plan to show potential accidents and make notes on what you have included to help create a safe environment.

Stretch

You are on placement in a preschool. Your supervisor has asked you to supervise the children in one of the activity areas, the creative area. Activities on offer include sand, water, play dough, painting at the easel, gluing with sequins and cutting.

1   Identify four potential accidents and explain how each accident might happen to a child in the creative area.

2   Describe the reasons why these accidents might happen in the creative area.

3   Explain how accidents can be prevented in the creative area.

Review your learning

Test your knowledge

1 Complete the sentences with the words below.

steam   oxygen   burn   lungs   cut   airway

a A sharp object can cause a _____.

b A scald is a type of _____ caused by very hot liquid or _____.

c Choking is caused when something blocks your _____ which prevents you from breathing.

d You will suffocate if the _____ supply to your _____ is cut off.

2 Complete the paragraph with the words below.

accidents   risk   harm   hazards   safe

Childcare settings must make regular _____ assessments to help keep the environment _____. They help you to be aware of potential _____ that could cause _____ to children, staff or visitors. This helps to lessen the risk of _____ happening.

What have you learnt?

	See section
• Plan to create a safe environment in a childcare setting.	1.1

Choosing suitable equipment for a childcare setting

Let's get started

Imagine you are setting up your own nursery. What equipment will you need? Where will the children sleep, eat and play? How will you decide what to buy?

Figure 2.10: Choosing suitable equipment

What will you learn?

- Essential equipment and factors for choice.

2.1 Essential equipment and factors for choice

Types of essential equipment

Let's start by thinking about the different situations in which equipment is used in childcare settings. Look at Figure 2.11.

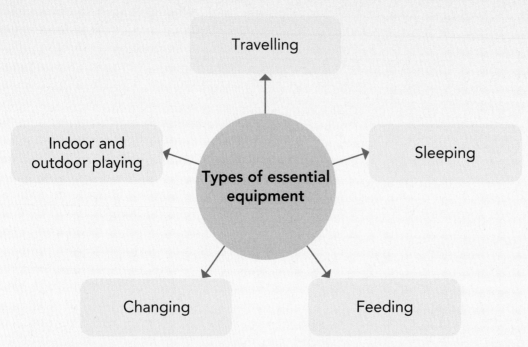

Figure 2.11: Types of essential equipment

Travelling

A childcare setting will need travelling equipment if they want to take the children for walks or outings. Travelling equipment includes prams, buggies and reins.

- Prams allow younger babies to lie flat until they can sit up unsupported, at around the age of six months.

- Buggies (also called pushchairs or strollers) will usually have a forward-facing seat so the child can look ahead. Some buggies have a reversible seat so the child can face you. If you are transporting two children, you can use a double buggy. A tandem buggy has one seat in front of the other, and a twin buggy has seats which are side by side.

- Reins can be used to help children stay safe on walks (see Figure 2.12). They are strapped to a child's body or wrist; this stops them running off or stepping into the road. Reins can offer support to babies and toddlers who are not very steady on their feet.

Figure 2.12: This toddler is out for a walk in the snow. How can the reins help to keep her safe?

Sleeping

Children need to sleep or rest at points throughout the day, so a setting needs sleeping equipment such as:

- cots, which are usually suitable for babies to sleep in up until the age of two
- rest mats, which are often used for older children sleeping in childcare settings – the mat is placed on the floor and covered with a sheet and a blanket
- bean bags, which are suitable for children aged over 12 months to rest on.

Feeding

A childcare setting needs feeding equipment to use at meal and snack times. When drinking, babies and young children may use trainer cups; Table 2.3 shows the different types.

Table 2.3: Types of trainer cup

Type of cup	Features
Sippy cup	Beaker-style cup with a spout or straw, with a non-spill valve
Free-flow beaker	Beaker with a free-flow valve
Doidy cup	A slanted cup, designed to help children learn to sip from the rim of a cup
Open cup	Open-top cups can be used from six months, with support

Bibs are often worn at mealtimes to protect children's clothes. Sectioned plates are suitable for babies who are weaning, as food can be divided up on the plate.

Changing

You will need to change babies' nappies regularly to keep them clean and comfortable, and to help prevent nappy rash.

Babies and children can be placed on changing mats. The safest place to change a baby's nappy is on a changing mat on the floor. However, this can put a strain on your back and knees, and many childcare settings use a changing table or changing station, so you can stand up when nappy changing.

You will also need changing equipment when you take babies and children on walks or outings. Items can be stored in a changing bag.

Indoor and outdoor playing

Babies and children need plenty of fresh air and space to be active; they need time to play outdoors as well as indoors. Sometimes, simply moving a piece of equipment to a different area can spark the children's interest in it. Childcare settings may use equipment which is suitable for indoor and outdoor playing, as shown in Figure 2.13.

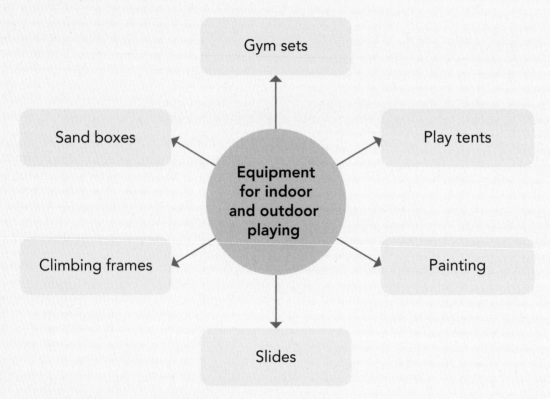

Figure 2.13: Equipment for indoor and outdoor playing

Let's get practical!   1

Think about resources for inside and outside playing. Research one or more pieces of equipment that would be suitable for both indoor and outdoor use, for each of the following age groups:

- babies under one year of age
- children aged one to three years
- children aged three to five years.

Over to you! 1

Match the pieces of equipment to their purpose in a childcare setting.

1	cot	a	travelling
2	buggy	b	sleeping
3	changing mat	c	feeding
4	slide	d	changing
5	sectioned plate	e	indoor and outdoor playing

Factors affecting suitability and choice

Imagine you are choosing a new sand box for indoor and outdoor playing in a childcare setting. If you type 'buy sand box' into a search engine, over 300 million results come up! How would you decide which is the best one to buy? There are many factors to consider when choosing suitable equipment. Table 2.4 summarises the questions you might ask to help you to decide if a piece of equipment is suitable.

Table 2.4: Factors affecting suitability and choice

Factor	Suggested questions to ask
Age and weight appropriateness	What age group is this piece of equipment suitable for?
	Are there minimum/maximum weight limits? What are they?
Safety	Is this equipment safe?
	What are the safety features?
	Is there a safety star rating? What is it?
	Does it have safety labelling?
	Is it stable?
	Is it flammable?
Design	Is this product comfortable, for both you and the child?
	Is the product accessible to children with special educational needs or disabilities (SEND)?
	Is it easy to use?
	Does it look attractive to the children and/or the staff?
	Can it be adjusted if needed?
	Can it be easily cleaned?
	Is it practical?

Table 2.4: Continued

Factor	Suggested questions to ask
Durability	Is the equipment hard-wearing?
	Will the materials withstand wear and tear?
	Is the equipment weatherproof if it will be used outdoors?
Cost	Is this item value for money?
	Is it in my price range?

By working through the questions, you might decide to reject a piece of equipment for one or more reasons. Let's look at the factors for choice in more detail.

Age and weight appropriateness

When choosing any piece of equipment, always check and follow the manufacturer's recommendations for age and weight appropriateness.

Some equipment, such as prams or changing tables, is only suitable for children up to a certain age or weight. If you ignore the manufacturer's recommendations and, for example, use a changing table with a child who is too heavy for it, the child might not be safe. Always check age advice symbols on any equipment before you use it to ensure it is suitable. See Unit R057, TA4, Section 4.3 for more information about safety labelling.

Safety

When choosing equipment, you must make sure it is safe. Research the safety features, star ratings and safety labelling, for example:

- If you are choosing a pram for travelling, make sure it has good quality brakes.

- If you are buying sectioned plates for feeding, check the plastic is chemical-free.

- If you are choosing a pop-up tent for inside and outside play, make sure it is made from non-flammable materials.

Equipment can be tested for safety and rated by experts who share their findings in consumer publications. It is the law that babies and young children use a car seat when travelling by car; these are tested for safety and awarded a star rating, with five stars being the best.

Let's get practical!   2

Search on the internet for 'baby buggy'.

Write down the cost of the cheapest and the most expensive model you can find.

1   Choose one of the buggies to research. Identify at least two safety features of your chosen buggy.

2   Would you recommend this buggy to your supervisor? Justify your answer.

Design

There is lots to think about when considering the design of a piece of equipment.

Comfort is important; babies and children must feel relaxed and comfortable when lying on changing mats, resting on bean bags or wearing bibs. Think about your own comfort too; for example, if choosing a changing bag, you may decide to choose one with a padded strap so it doesn't dig into you. You may prefer a buggy with handles that can be adjusted depending on your height.

Take into account **accessibility** and the individual needs of the children who will be using the equipment. You should consider children's special educational needs and disabilities and choose equipment that can be used by children of different abilities. Adaptive utensils, such as cutlery with comfort grip handles or a curved design, can support children with limited motor skills to eat independently. Sensory resources, like textured balls or **balance** cushions, can be used by children with autism for indoor and outdoor playing.

Think about how easy equipment is to use. For example, if you are choosing a buggy for nursery outings, make sure it is easy to fold up and easy to open and that fingers won't get trapped – yours or the children's.

When choosing equipment, you may want to think about aesthetics (how something looks). Children might be happy to use an open cup if they like the colour, or they may be excited to use the gym set if it looks fun and attractive. Remember to be practical though; don't choose equipment based only on how it looks.

Some equipment that childcare settings use is adjustable, which means you can adapt it to meet the needs of the babies or children present. An example would be a climbing frame where the height can be adjusted depending on the age of the children using it, or a trainer cup, where the lid can be removed to change it from a beaker to an open cup. Adjustable equipment is useful as it can be adapted as children's needs change.

Durability

Equipment in childcare settings is likely to get a lot of use! Think about how often children play on a slide, or how many times a day a changing table is used. For this reason, choose equipment that is hard-wearing. There is no point spending money on a piece of equipment that will wear out quickly. Check that materials are **durable** and equipment is sturdy.

Let's get practical!   3

Use the internet to search buying options for 'changing mats'. Choose one changing mat and work through the questions below.

- Is the mat wipeable and easy to clean?
- Is it waterproof?
- Is the material non-toxic?
- Will the baby be safe?
- Does the mat seem durable?
- Will the baby be comfortable?
- Is the mat affordable?

1. What are two positive points about the changing mat you researched?

2. Did the changing mat you researched seem durable? Explain your decision.

3. Would you recommend this changing mat? Justify your answer.

Cost

Cost is a factor that childcare settings need to think about when buying equipment. Look for items that are good **value for money** so you are not paying a higher price than the equipment is worth. Choose equipment that is within the price range that the childcare setting is willing to spend. Often settings have a budget that they need to stick to.

Over to you!   2

Your supervisor has a meeting scheduled with a furniture salesperson to buy some new highchairs for the nursery.

Safety and durability are the main priorities (most important things). The highchairs need to be easy to clean and will need to be folded away after use. Your supervisor wants to secure the best price she can.

List five questions that your supervisor could ask the furniture salesperson in order to find a suitable highchair.

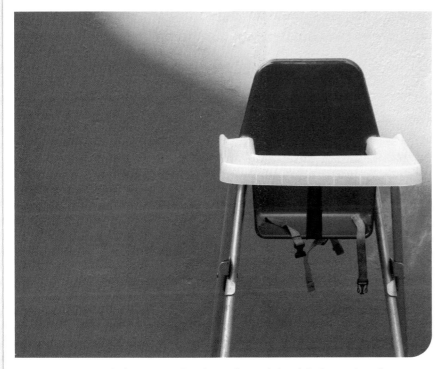

Figure 2.14: Highchairs need to be safe and durable but other factors need to be considered too

You have now looked at the factors affecting suitability and choice. Let's link these factors to the essential equipment needed in a childcare setting.

Travelling

A key feature of a pram is that it allows a baby to lie flat. This is both a design and a safety feature because babies need to lie flat to protect their spines, even when they're not sleeping. A pram is usually suitable until a baby can sit up unsupported, at around the age of six months.

Durability and cost factors will depend on the situation. A childcare setting may get lots of use out of a pram as new children join. It may want to buy an expensive pram to make sure it lasts for a long time.

As you can see in Figure 2.15, some buggies have a flexible design, which means they can be adjusted to meet the needs of growing children. They have a seat that can fully recline (lie flat), which means they can be used from birth. Later on, the seat can be moved to an upright position for older babies. The length of the seat and height of the leg rest can be adjusted to accommodate different heights and ages of children. A buggy will usually have a forward-facing seat so the child can look ahead. Some buggies have a reversible seat so the child can face you. A buggy made with a hard-wearing material that is easy to clean is important for durability.

Buggies can have three or four wheels, depending on the design; some have swivel front wheels which can be locked for safety if you are pushing the buggy on a bumpy path. The height of the handles may be adjustable. You must always strap children in using a five-point harness to keep them safe and secure.

A more expensive sturdy design may be more comfortable for the child for longer periods of use, and the seat may be padded for the child's comfort. A good suspension system can stop a baby being bounced around too much.

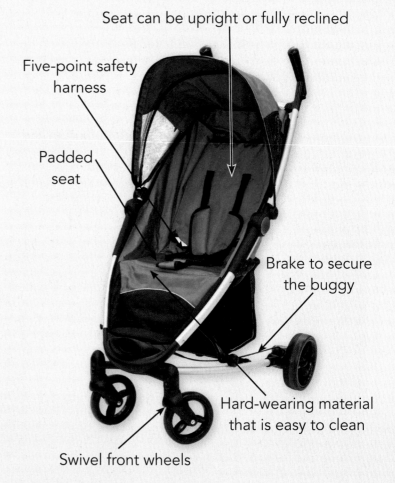

Seat can be upright or fully reclined

Five-point safety harness

Padded seat

Brake to secure the buggy

Hard-wearing material that is easy to clean

Swivel front wheels

Figure 2.15: Key features of a buggy

You must use the brake when you stop a pram or buggy; it is important that the brake works well and is easy to use.

Buggies can come with a range of extra features, including parasols (to shade children from the sun) and rain covers. Buggies with more features usually cost more money than those with a basic design.

Always check that a buggy is stable (not likely to tip over) before you use it. A low cost, lightweight buggy can easily tip backwards if you hang a bag on the back of it. However, if you travel by bus with the children in your care, a large, bulky buggy might not be practical.

When considering reins, safety is the main priority, as well as making sure the child is comfortable wearing them. The design may play a part, as children might be happier to wear reins if they double up as a small backpack that they can put a toy in.

Stretch

On your placement at a day nursery, you have been asked to research options for a new buggy. The buggy will be used to take the babies and toddlers out on walks in the local area.

Explain the factors to consider when deciding which buggy would be suitable and evaluate why each factor is important.

Sleeping

Choosing suitable sleeping equipment is very important. (For information about how to help prevent SIDS, see R057, Topic Area 3, Section 3.2.)

Cots must conform to British Safety Standards BS EN 716; this means that the cot meets the required safety standards, for example the space between the bars should be no more than 6.5 cm so the baby cannot get stuck in the gaps. (See Figure 2.16.)

Figure 2.16: Why must childcare settings buy equipment that conforms to British Safety Standards?

To ensure safety, the cot must have a mattress that fits with no gaps – otherwise the baby could get stuck between the mattress and the side of the cot. Check the mattress is clean and dry with no rips before using it. The distance between the top of the mattress and the top of the cot must be at least 50 cm; a baby may climb over and fall if the sides are not high enough.

Table 2.5: Types of cot and their features

Type of cot	Features
Standard cot	Most cots are rectangular in shape and are usually made of wood or MDF (an engineered wood product).
Adjustable cot	Some cots have height-adjustable bases, so as the baby grows and becomes more mobile you can lower the base to prevent them climbing out.
Drop side cot	Drop side cots let you lower one or both sides, making it easier to lift the baby in and out. You should check that the moving parts are in good working order so the baby does not get trapped.
Cot bed	Cot beds allow the sides and one end to be removed (taken off) to create a junior bed. They are larger than standard sized cots and can be used for children aged up to around eight years old.
Evacuation cots	Evacuation cots are on wheels and are found in some day nurseries. When there is a fire drill, babies can be placed in the cot and wheeled out to the assembly point.
Travel cots	Travel cots can be folded down and stored in a bag. They have a plastic or metal frame, mesh sides, and a lightly padded mattress.

A childcare setting may use rest mats or beanbags for older children to sleep or rest on; they should be made of durable material if they will be getting a lot of use. A useful design feature of some rest mats is that they can be folded away after use to save space. Remember, for safety, bean bags are not suitable for babies under 12 months old due to the risk of suffocation.

Feeding

From six months of age, babies can be offered water from a cup (see Figure 2.17). Free-flow beakers or open cups are advised as they help the baby learn to sip, rather than suck; beakers with non-spill valves help to prevent spills but are not recommended.

Children who are weaning may benefit from sectioned plates; the design means food is separated and they often have higher sides to

Figure 2.17: Beakers and cups are usually made of plastic or silicone and can come with or without handles.

reduce spills. You should clean feeding equipment after every use. If the childcare setting uses a dishwasher, items that are dishwasher safe are required. Plastic equipment can become scratched and harbour **bacteria**, so throw it away if this happens. Check that any products you choose are free from chemicals; look out for phthalate-free, latex-free and BPA-free materials.

When babies are weaning and as children become more independent at feeding themselves, it can get quite messy! Bibs can be made of waterproof materials to prevent food stains and stop babies from feeling wet and uncomfortable.

Let's get practical!   4

Design a survey for family and friends who are parents or who care for babies in order to gather information about bibs.

Write five or more questions to find out about the types of bibs they use and the factors that influence their choice.

Use your survey results to help you decide on a suitable bib to recommend for use in a childcare setting.

Over to you!   3

Read the statements. Are they true or false?

a   Free-flow beakers help babies to learn the skill of sipping, rather than sucking.

b   Sippy cups are best in nurseries; they prevent spills and stop the floor getting slippery and dangerous.

c   Children should use cups made of glass as plastic ones can contain chemicals.

d   Sectioned plates can be used to support weaning.

Changing

Changing mats help to make nappy changing safe and comfortable for babies, so it is important to consider factors such as design and materials. If using a changing table, make sure it is a sturdy design and suitable for the weight of the children being changed. Childcare settings may choose changing tables with safety rails, or tables that are height-adjustable.

Changings bags are needed when taking children out of the setting. The size of the bag may depend on how much nappy changing equipment is needed, for example tubs of cream or lots of changes of clothes if a child is potty training. You should find a bag that is suitable for you to carry – you may want a backpack if you are walking or a bag with pram clips if pushing a buggy. Some bags have special design features, like built-in changing mats, padded straps or extra compartments.

> **Let's get practical!   5**
>
> Design your own ideal changing bag.
>
> Label three or more features of your design to explain why your bag would be a good choice for use in a playgroup.

Indoor and outdoor playing

Childcare settings may buy equipment that can be used both inside and out; this is a good way of managing their budget. Equipment should be safe and easy to move between the inside and outside areas. If a piece of equipment is to be left outside for any length of time then it needs to be durable to cope with the weather conditions. A hard-wearing material, such as a treated wood, may be more expensive to buy but should last longer. Safety is a key consideration for any piece of play equipment, especially one that is designed to be left outside.

Case study

Choosing equipment – Jorge decides

The local gym offers a crèche for children aged six months to five years. The supervisor, Jorge, wants to buy a new waterplay table to use during inside and outside play. It must be safe for all the babies and children to use and easy for the staff to move.

Jorge looks in the *KidsPlay* catalogue and places an order for the Basics Waterplay Table.

KidsPlay Waterplay Tables			
	Basics Waterplay Table £19.99	Pirate Waterplay Table £29.99	Splash! Waterplay Table £79.99
Age range	6 months +	3 years +	6 months +
Safety warnings	To be used under the direct supervision of an adult	To be used under the direct supervision of an adult Not suitable for children under 36 months due to small parts	To be used under the direct supervision of an adult Caution: Heavy item
Design and features	Easy assembly Portable	Easy assembly Portable Includes two toy pirates, anchor and water cannon	Two-person assembly required Sturdy, hard-wearing design

Figure 2.18: KidsPlay catalogue

Check your understanding

1 State one factor that might have influenced Jorge's decision to buy the Basics Waterplay Table.

2 Identify one factor that made the Pirate Waterplay Table unsuitable.

3 Jorge rejected the Splash! Waterplay Table. Explain why. Give at least two reasons.

Review your learning

Test your knowledge

Choose the best answer for each question below:

1 What type of factors are comfort, ease of use, adjustability and accessibility?

   A cost   B design   C safety

2 What factors might you consider when choosing equipment that is safe?

   A star ratings   B aesthetics   C price range

3 Which factor relates to how hard-wearing a piece of equipment is?

   A design

   B age and weight appropriateness

   C durability

4 Which factor should you consider when choosing equipment within a set price range?

   A design   B durability   C cost

What have you learnt?

	See section
• Essential equipment and factors for choice.	2.1

Nutritional needs of children from birth to five years

Let's get started   1

What does 'nutritional needs' mean? Why do people check food labels?

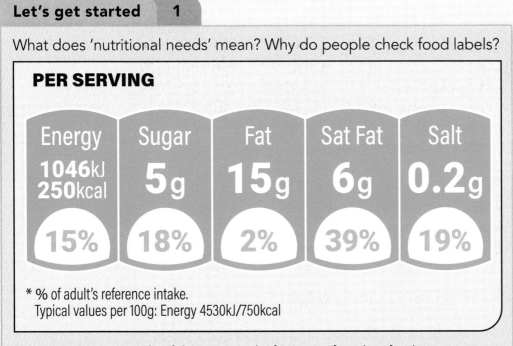

PER SERVING

Energy	Sugar	Fat	Sat Fat	Salt
1046kJ **250**kcal	**5**g	**15**g	**6**g	**0.2**g
15%	18%	2%	39%	19%

* % of adult's reference intake.
  Typical values per 100g: Energy 4530kJ/750kcal

Figure 2.19: An example of the nutritional information found on food items

What will you learn?

- Current government dietary recommendations for healthy eating for children from birth to five years.

- Essential nutrients and their functions for children from birth to five years.

- Planning for preparing a feed/meal.

- How to evaluate planning and preparation of a feed/meal.

3.1 Current government dietary recommendations for healthy eating for children from birth to five years

'Diet' means the food you usually eat. The UK Government recommends different foods and drinks that provide a healthy, **balanced diet**.

Eatwell Guide

The UK Government has produced the Eatwell Guide. It shows how different foods and drinks can contribute to healthy eating habits. Adults and children aged two years and over should follow the Eatwell Guide (see Figure 2.20). (Note that the Eatwell Guide does not apply to children aged under two as they have different nutritional needs. Later in this topic area, you will learn about healthy diets for babies and children aged under two years.)

Five a day

The Change4Life campaign, which was produced by Public Health England (PHE), aims to help families lead healthier lives by eating well. (PHE is a government agency that works to improve the nation's health.) One recommendation is that adults and children should eat at least five portions of fruit and vegetables every day. A portion is approximately the amount of food an adult or child can fit into the palm of their hand.

Adults and children need to eat a variety of fruit and vegetables. Imagine 'eating the rainbow', as fruit and vegetables of different colours contain different **nutrients**. Fruit and vegetables can be fresh, tinned or frozen. They can be found in soups, sauces and drinks. However, pure fruit juice, vegetable juice and smoothies only count as a maximum of one of your five a day, no matter how much you drink.

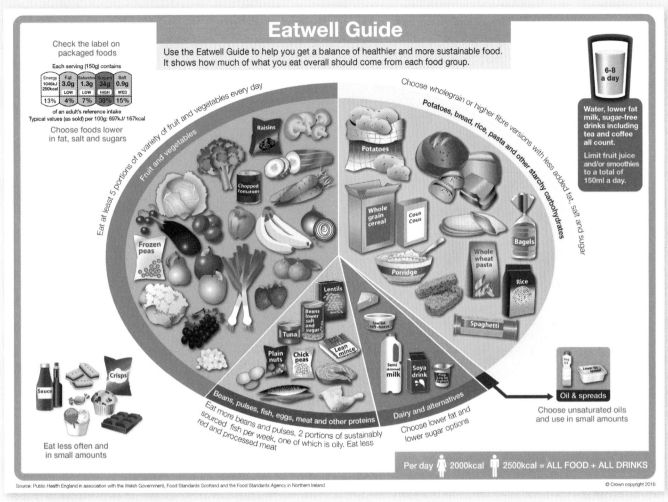

Figure 2.20: The Eatwell Guide divides foods and drinks into five food groups and gives recommendations for a balanced diet

| Let's get practical! | 1 |

Keep a food diary for a week. Are you getting your five a day?

British Nutrition Foundation recommendations

The British Nutrition Foundation (BNF) is a registered charity. It gives advice and information about healthy eating and nutrition, which mirror the principles of the Eatwell Guide.

The BNF has published a guide for healthy eating for children aged one to four years, called '5532-a-day'. It recommends that children eat five portions of starchy foods, five or more portions of fruit and vegetables, three portions of dairy foods and two portions of protein foods (or three portions if a child is vegetarian). It also recommends appropriate portion sizes. See Figure 2.21.

Figure 2.21: The 5532-a-day guide

Future recommendations

The government and groups like the British Nutrition Foundation are constantly researching and investigating nutrition and healthy diets. It is a good idea to keep up to date with recommendations and be aware of developments in the future.

Applying the dietary recommendations for healthy eating

Eating a balanced diet helps children to take in the wide range of nutrients their bodies need to stay healthy and to function.

Portion control is one way the government recommends that children stay healthy. We all have different appetites and require different amounts of energy (calories) from food to stay fit and well.

To stay a healthy weight, children should only eat as much food as their bodies need. Being overweight can lead to **obesity** – this means being very overweight with too much body fat. If portion sizes are too big, children will eat more calories than they need. Look again at Figure 2.20 which shows the portion sizes recommended by the BNF for children aged one to four.

There are government guidelines as to how many calories children and adults should generally take in to maintain a healthy weight. A two-year-old girl needs about 1000 calories a day. One takeaway burger can contain over 1000 calories! Table 2.6 shows the recommended daily calories for male and female children aged between one year old and six years old.

Table 2.6: Recommended calorie intake for children of different ages

Age (years)	1		2–3		4–6	
Sex	M	F	M	F	M	F
Calories	765	717	1088	1004	1482	1378

The government recommends that adults limit the amount of processed foods, fast food and snacks children eat. (Processed foods are those that have been made or packaged for you, usually for convenience. They often have extra fat, salt or sugar added to them.) For example:

- A microwave meal, such as vegetable chilli, is processed food. A healthier choice would be to offer a child a homemade vegetable chilli using fresh ingredients.

- Sausages and bacon are examples of processed meats; they can be very salty. Limit the amount that you give to children. Too much salt can raise blood pressure, increasing the risk of a child having a stroke or a heart attack in later life.

- Fast foods, like pizza and takeaways, are heavily processed and should only be offered to children occasionally.

- Snacks like chocolate bars or crisps should be eaten less often and in small amounts. Encourage children to eat healthy meals and snacks; fruit is a healthy snack choice.

- At mealtimes, offer lots of colourful vegetables.

- Encourage children to be involved in making healthy meals as this helps to foster healthy eating habits.

Over to you!   1

Look at the following snacks. They all include fruit or vegetables, but can you suggest a healthier alternative for each option?

a   Raspberry-flavoured yoghurt

b   Slice of carrot cake

c   Apple and raisin cereal bar

Let's get practical!   2

Making healthy foods look attractive, interesting and fun is a great way to make them appealing to children. For example, you can arrange a fruit salad to look like a flower or display vegetables on a plate to make a face.

Draw a 'plate' on a piece of paper (or use a paper plate). Decide on a healthy meal and draw it on the plate. Make the food look as exciting as possible!

The government recommends that adults limit the amount of sugar, fat and salt that children eat. Look back at the Eatwell Guide; you will see that it suggests choosing foods lower in sugar, fat and salt. Here are some ideas:

- Don't add extra sugar or salt to children's food.

- Check food labels – some foods, like breakfast cereals or yoghurts, have high amounts of sugar or salt.

- Offer children **unsaturated** rather than **saturated fats**. Saturated fats usually come from animals. They are found in foods like cheese, ice cream, sausages and chocolate. Too much saturated fat can lead to obesity. The oils found in plants and fish tend to be unsaturated fats, which are a healthier choice.

- From two years of age, offer children semi-skimmed rather than full fat milk, and reduced fat rather than full fat cheese. Low-fat options are not recommended for children aged under two because fat is essential for babies' brain development, and the calories in fat provide the fuel needed for babies to grow.

- To help cut down on fat, offer children over two years of age lean cuts of meat, cut the fat off meat and take the skin off chicken. Grill, bake, steam, boil or poach food, rather than frying it.

- Encourage children to brush their teeth regularly to keep them clean and healthy.

Limit fizzy drinks and fruit juice. Fizzy drinks often have sugar added to them. Fruit juice contains lots of natural sugars. Too much sugar can lead to obesity and tooth decay. Tooth decay is when the hard outer layer of the tooth, called enamel, is damaged. Bacteria can then attack a child's teeth, causing pain and even tooth loss. Never put drinks such as fruit juice or squash in a baby's bottle as this can cause tooth decay.

Water, low-fat milk (from aged two) and sugar-free drinks are healthier alternatives to fizzy drinks and fruit juice. Encourage children to drink six to eight cups of water a day. For children under five years old, the cup should be between 120 ml and 150 ml.

In some cases, young children may have an intolerance or food allergy. In this situation their parents should always speak to their GP or health visitor.

Stretch

Millie is five. This is what Millie eats and drinks on most days:

- Breakfast: jam and butter on toast
- Lunch: ham sandwich and a bag of crisps
- Dinner: baked beans on buttered toast, followed by ice cream
- Snacks: chocolate biscuits or sweets
- Drinks: lemonade, cola or fizzy orange

1 If Millie carries on eating and drinking like this every day, explain how this might affect:

   a her teeth

   b her weight

   c her health in the future.

2 Describe an alternative breakfast and lunch choice for Millie. Justify your choice and explain how the foods you have chosen meet government dietary recommendations.

Test your knowledge   1

The Eatwell Guide is recommended for children aged over two. It shows the five food groups and how much food per day should come from each group.

1   State the two food groups that most of a child's food should come from in a day.

2   State the food group that is represented by the small purple section.

3   State the food group that contains milk and yoghurt.

4   State one food that the government recommends children eat less of.

3.2 Essential nutrients and their functions for children from birth to five years

Let's get started   3

Look at these essential nutrients. What role do you think each of these nutrients plays in helping children to stay healthy?

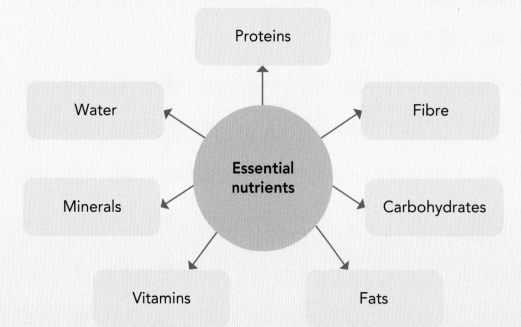

Figure 2.22: Essential nutrients to help children stay healthy

Children's bodies are amazing! In the first year, their brains double in size. By the age of five, children have usually doubled in height. They can fight off infections and recover from injuries and illnesses. They have the energy to move in all sorts of ways, they get stronger and stay alert.

Let's look in more detail at the essential nutrients children need and their functions (what they do). Children need proteins, carbohydrates and fats in large amounts to stay healthy. They need vitamins and minerals in smaller amounts.

Proteins

Proteins are needed for growth and repair. If a child does not eat enough protein, they will not grow properly. Children need protein to recover from illness or injury as it allows the body to repair itself.

Sources of protein include: beans, pulses, fish, eggs, meat, tofu, nuts, milk and dairy products.

Carbohydrates

Carbohydrates are needed to produce energy. Children need energy to stay active and alert throughout the day.

Sources of carbohydrates include: potatoes, bread, rice, pasta and cereals.

Fats

Fats are needed for warmth and protection. Babies and children need to keep warm; the fat on their bodies helps to shield them against the cold. It also acts as a protective layer around their internal organs, such as the heart and liver.

Sources of fats include: butter, oil, nuts, avocado, oily fish.

Vitamins

Children need a variety of vitamins for good health and to prevent diseases. Figure 2.23 shows the functions of essential vitamins and Table 2.7 shows the sources of these vitamins.

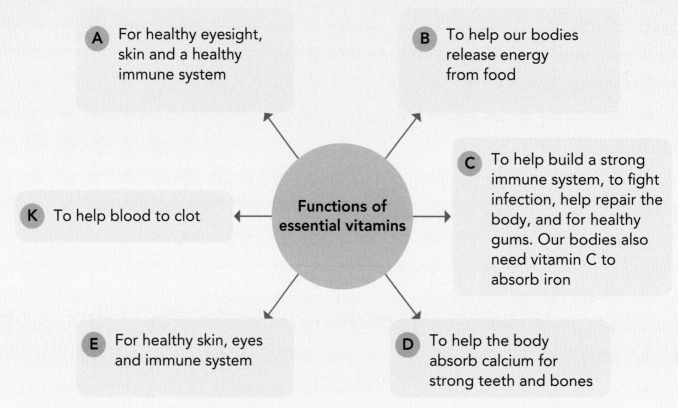

Figure 2.23: Functions of essential vitamins

Table 2.7: Sources of essential vitamins

Vitamin	Food source
Vitamin A	Liver, eggs, milk, dairy foods, orange-coloured fruits, sweet potatoes, carrots and leafy green vegetables
Vitamin B	Fortified breakfast cereals (the vitamin is added by the manufacturer), nuts, meat, milk, dairy foods
Vitamin C	Blackcurrants, blueberries, kiwi, mango, orange, pineapple, broccoli, chilli, kale, peppers, Brussels sprouts
Vitamin D	Fortified breakfast cereals, eggs, meat, oily fish, margarine
Vitamin E	Nuts, seeds
Vitamin K	Leafy green vegetables

Minerals

Minerals are needed for strong bones and teeth, to make red blood cells, to heal wounds and for a strong **immune system**. Calcium, iron and zinc are essential minerals for children. Figure 2.24 shows their functions.

Calcium

For strong teeth and bones, to help the blood clot and for normal nerve and muscle function

Iron

To help make red blood cells which carry oxygen around our bodies

To prevent anaemia, a condition which can make you feel very tired

Zinc

To help wounds heal, to make new cells and to process proteins, carbohydrates and fats

Figure 2.24: Functions of essential minerals

Table 2.8 shows sources of calcium, iron and zinc.

Table 2.8: Sources of essential minerals

Mineral	Food source
Calcium	Dairy foods, milk, green leafy vegetables, sardines, white bread, non-dairy milks fortified with calcium
Zinc	Red meat, liver, eggs, fish, green leafy vegetables, fortified breakfast cereals and wholegrains
Iron	Meat, shellfish, milk, dairy foods, wholegrains, bread

Let's get practical!   3

Create a survey to find out what your family and friends' favourite vegetable is. Research the most popular vegetable and identify one or more nutrients (vitamins and minerals) it provides.

Fibre

Fibre (also known as roughage) is needed for a healthy digestive system. Fibre cannot be absorbed by your gut, so eating fibre helps to prevent constipation.

Fibre can fill up small stomachs quickly, leaving less room for other foods rich in essential nutrients that young children need. Gradually start offering children more fibre from around the age of two. Fibre is not a nutrient, but it is an essential as part of a healthy balanced diet.

Good sources of fibre include: wholegrains (in cereals, pasta and bread), fruit (such as strawberries, pears, melon and oranges), vegetables (such as broccoli, carrots and sweetcorn) and baked potatoes.

Water

Children need water to stay hydrated – this means that the child's body has absorbed enough water. Water is needed for nearly every bodily function. Babies and children need to be hydrated to keep cool in hot weather and to digest their food. As with fibre, water is not a nutrient, but is it an essential as part of a healthy balanced diet.

Food sources to meet nutritional needs from birth to six months

Breast milk is the only food and drink babies need in the first six months of life. Research shows that breastfeeding protects babies from infections and diseases. If a baby is unable to be breast fed, then the alternative is formula milk (see Figure 2.25). Formula milk (also known as baby formula, **infant** formula or first milk) comes as a dry powder, which you make up with water, or as a ready-made liquid. The ready-made version tends to be more expensive.

Figure 2.25: What do young babies eat and drink? Do you think there is cow's milk in this bottle?

Formula milk provides all the nutrients that a baby needs to grow and develop. This includes protein, carbohydrates in the form of **lactose** (the milk sugar), fats, vitamins, (including A, C, D, E, K and the B vitamins) and minerals, such as iron, calcium and zinc.

Let's get practical!   4

Examine a tub of formula milk. Can you locate the nutrition facts on the label? Does it list all the essential nutrients that a baby needs?

Case study

A nanny's experience

Tara is a nanny for baby Emilia, aged 18 weeks. Emilia's mother was breastfeeding her, but she has gone back to work full time. Tara will need to start bottle-feeding Emilia.

Tara is asked to start Emilia on first infant formula. She decides to research a leading brand and identifies that it is:

Figure 2.26: Choosing the correct infant formula

- a suitable substitute for breast milk

- suitable from birth

- nutritionally complete – she checks the nutritional information on the tin.

Tara is concerned, as Emilia is bringing up milk straight after her feeds. Tara seeks advice from her health visitor who thinks Emilia is suffering from reflux. He recommends trying an anti-reflux formula.

Tara researches the recommended formula, and identifies that it is:

- suitable from birth

- thickened to help prevent reflux

- only to be used under the advice of a health professional.

Emilia starts on the anti-reflux formula and seems much more content; she is able to keep her feeds down.

Check your understanding

1 Describe why Tara was asked to offer Emilia first infant formula.

2 Outline what is meant by 'nutritionally complete'.

3 Explain why it was important to seek advice from the health visitor when Emilia started bringing up her feeds.

Food sources to meet nutritional needs for the three stages of weaning between 6 and 12 months

Figure 2.27: This baby is trying new foods. Do you like tasting new flavours? Are you happy to give different tastes and textures a try?

From around the age of six months, it is time to start introducing babies to food (see Figure 2.27). This process is called **weaning**. Weaning helps babies to start to take their nutrients from food, rather than only milk. Babies need to learn how to move food around their mouths and swallow it.

Weaning is a gradual process. Babies have tiny stomachs so offer small amounts of food at first. Introduce new foods and textures gradually. Some babies struggle initially with lumpy textures and may gag but keep on offering a range of foods. Some babies may be happier to feed themselves; this is called baby-led weaning.

As babies approach 12 months old, offer a wide range of tastes and textures from the different food groups. If you only offer sweet-tasting vegetables, like sweet potato or carrot, they might develop a 'sweet tooth'. Offering a wide range of flavours may help prevent them being fussy eaters as they get older. It will also help them to take in all the nutrients they need.

Weaning usually happens in three stages, as shown in Figure 2.28.

Weaning stage 1

- Try offering a couple of teaspoons of baby rice or baby cereal (mixed with their usual milk). These are good sources of carbohydrate which give the baby energy.

- Offer pureed vegetables or fruit. Broccoli, spinach and cauliflower can be easily blended, and are rich in vitamins and minerals, needed for a strong immune system.

Weaning stage 2

- After a couple of weeks, the next stage is to start offering lumpier textures. Mash, rather than puree, foods.

- Introduce options like minced chicken, for protein, and fingers of toast which are carbohydrates.

- Gradually introduce 'finger foods' such as soft sticks of cooked potato, parsnip, yam, apple or pear.

- Babies will start to have three small meals per day as well as their usual milk feeds.

Weaning stage 3

- By around ten months old, babies need three meals every day and will start to reduce the amount of milk feeds they are having.

- Introduce foods such as pasta for energy, pieces of cheese for protein and fat, and continue offering babies lots of fruit and veg.

- Babies can start to drink unsweetened fruit juice and water. This helps to keep them hydrated.

Figure 2.28: The three stages of weaning, from six months old

Over to you!   2

Imagine you are caring for an 11-month-old baby. Complete the shopping list below, adding one more food option to each nutrient group.

- *Carbohydrates: oat cakes, potatoes*

- *Proteins: lentils, canned fish*

- *Fats: cheese triangles, full fat yoghurt*

- *Vitamins: blueberries, peppers*

- *Minerals: milk, Brussels sprouts*

Food sources to meet nutritional needs for children aged one to five years

From one year old, children need three meals and two healthy snacks per day. At this stage, children should eat food from all the main food groups. From two years old, children can start to follow the Eatwell Guide principles (which differ slightly from the BFN's 5532-a-day guide).

Bread, cereals, potatoes and rice are all carbohydrates. These provide children with energy as well as some nutrients and fibre. Wholegrain versions of pasta, rice and bread should not be given too often to children under two as they are high in fibre and may fill them up before they have had enough nutrients. After two years of age, more fibre can be offered.

Fruit and vegetables are a child's main source of vitamins, minerals and fibre. It is important to include fruit and vegetables at every meal so that children become used to eating them and learn the importance of eating healthily. A variety should be included as much as possible, as different fruits and vegetables contain the range of vitamins and minerals their bodies need to grow and develop.

From 12 months old, formula milk can be replaced with whole cow's milk. Offer this from a free-flow or open cup, rather than a bottle. From two years of age, lower-fat options are recommended so whole milk can be replaced with semi-skimmed milk. Milk and dairy products are a good source of calcium, which is good for the child's developing bones and teeth. They also contain vitamin A, which helps the body to fight infections as well as helping the development of healthy eyes and skin.

Pulses, beans, fish, eggs and meat contain iron as well as protein. This is important as it supports healthy growth and development. If a child is vegetarian or vegan, they need to have three portions of protein foods a day. Meat-free substitutes such as soya and tofu are also good sources of protein and iron.

Nuts are a good source of vitamin E, fat and protein. Remember! Never give whole nuts to a child under the age of five, as they are a choking hazard. Smooth nut butters (like smooth peanut butter) or ground nuts (like pine nuts in pesto) can be introduced from six months old.

Over to you!   3

Meat and fish are good sources of protein. If a child is vegetarian or vegan, then they do not eat meat or fish.

a   List three meat-free foods that provide protein.

b   Explain why children need protein as part of a balanced diet.

Following the BFN 5532-a-day guide and the Eatwell Guide will ensure young children eat a range of foods that provide them with all the essential nutrients needed.

Test your knowledge   2

Choose the correct word to complete the sentences:

1   Potatoes, bread, rice and pasta are sources of **fat / carbohydrate**; they provide us with energy.

2   Our bodies need protein for repair and **hydration / growth**. Protein is found in beans, pulses, meat, fish, eggs and dairy products.

3   **Calcium / Fat**, found in oils and spreads, provides our bodies with energy, helps to keep us warm and protects our internal organs.

4   Vitamins help to keep our bodies healthy. They help to build a strong **blood / immune** system.

5   **Minerals / Proteins** are nutrients that help to keep our bodies working properly. Examples include calcium, zinc and iron.

6   We need **fibre / fat** in our diets to help to keep food moving through the digestive system.

7   Water is essential in our diet to keep our bodies **hydrated / clean**.

3.3 Planning for preparing a feed/meal

What equipment do you need to make a bottle feed? Will any powdered milk do? Does it matter how many scoops you put in?

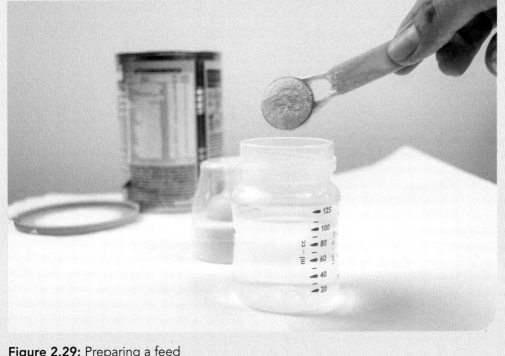

Figure 2.29: Preparing a feed

Equipment

When planning feeds and meals for babies and children, you need to make sure you are meeting their nutritional needs. You also need to think about the equipment you will need. You will need the following equipment to make a formula feed:

- steriliser
- bottle
- kettle
- scoop (provided with the powdered formula)
- flat-bladed knife (or leveller provided with the powdered formula).

Up until the age of 12 months, you must **sterilise** babies' feeding equipment, a process that kills bacteria. Milk is a perfect breeding-ground for bacteria, so you must sterilise breast pumps, bottles and teats; babies are less able to fight off infections caused by bacteria, like diarrhoea and vomiting (being sick).

Table 2.9 shows some common methods to sterilise equipment.

Table 2.9: Methods of sterilisation

Type of sterilisation	Method
Cold water sterilising solution	A sterilising tablet is placed in a tank of cold water. A lid is placed on so equipment is fully submerged (held under water) for 30 minutes to kill bacteria.
Steam sterilising	Equipment is placed in an electric sterilising unit or a microwave sterilising unit and the steam produced kills the bacteria.
Boiling	Items are placed in a large pan of boiling water and boiled for ten minutes. The equipment must be fully submerged to kill the bacteria.

Bottles are used to feed babies under 12 months of age. Standard baby bottles are narrow and cylinder shaped, others are shorter and wider, and some are oval shaped with a hole in the middle, to help the baby hold their own bottle.

Each bottle will need a latex or silicone teat for the baby to suck on. Teats can be shaped like a bell or a nipple. The size of the hole in the teat will let the milk flow at different rates. Only expressed breast milk or formula milk should be offered from a bottle.

Figure 2.30 shows the different parts of a baby's bottle.

There are lots of types of equipment that you may need to prepare a meal. Before you start making a meal, check you have all the equipment ready. For example, if you are preparing fruit or vegetables, you may need a knife or a peeler. You might need scales, a measuring jug or measuring spoons if you need to weigh or measure out ingredients.

Let's get practical!   5

Create a poster or presentation identifying and describing the equipment you will need to make a meal of your choice.

Figure 2.30: The parts of a baby's bottle

Ingredients and quantities

The ingredients needed to make a bottle feed are formula powder and water. You learnt about the different types of infant formula in Section 3.2. The water must be fresh from the tap, not bottled water. You must boil the water using a kettle as this kills any bacteria that could make the baby ill.

The tin or tub of formula you use will tell you the quantities of formula powder and water needed to make up the feed. It is important to make up formula feeds accurately, to keep the baby healthy and well.

- If a feed is too thick, the baby may become dehydrated or constipated (unable to poo easily).
- If a feed is too weak, the baby will not get the right quantity of nutrients.

Before you give a baby a **bottle feed**, you must check the milk is at the right temperature. It will be too hot when it is freshly made. You can test the temperature by putting a few drops of the milk on your wrist – you will be able to feel if it is too hot. To cool a bottle down, place it in a jug of cold water.

Let's get practical!   6

Research using the internet and then design a leaflet explaining how to safely make a formula feed.

In Section 3.2, you learnt about healthy meals and snacks for children, and the types of foods that meet their nutritional needs. When planning a meal, choose healthy ingredients and remember to offer a **balance** of foods across the five food groups. You can refer to the BNF 5532-a-day guide to portion sizes in Section 3.1.

If you are following a recipe, this will list the ingredients needed. Make sure you have them all ready before you start. You need to measure them out accurately, or the recipe might go wrong.

Let's get practical!   7

Research a suitable meal or snack for a baby who is weaning that could be served in a nursery. Create a recipe card, listing the ingredients and the quantities needed.

Safety

Accidents can happen in food preparation areas. Here are ways you can stay safe when you are making feeds or meals.

- Pick up knives by the handle and carry them with the blade tip facing down. Cut downwards and away from yourself. Take care with scissors, graters and peelers with sharp edges. Store knives safely, for example in a knife block.

- Always follow food safety guidelines. Use different coloured chopping boards to prepare certain foods, for example a red board for raw meat and a green board for vegetables. Make sure cloths and tea towels are clean, so you are not spreading germs around.

- Mop up any spillages straight away so you don't slip on a wet floor.

- Take care with electrical and hot appliances. Kettles can cause burns; boiling water and steam can scald you. Make sure your hands are dry before plugging in the kettle or any other electrical equipment. Make sure the handles of pans on the hob are not sticking out and use oven gloves if handling hot dishes.

Food hygiene

Food poisoning can be caused by eating food which has touched germs and is contaminated with bacteria. It can make you extremely ill. To help stop bacteria from spreading, you must do the following:

- Disinfect the worktop before you start – you can use an antibacterial spray. Keep the food preparation area clean. Wipe up spills straight away and wipe down and disinfect surfaces as you use them.

- Use hot water and detergent (washing-up liquid) to wash up equipment.

- Clean utensils and chopping boards as you go along. Use a separate chopping board for raw meat (a red one if possible). You don't want bacteria from raw meat to contaminate other foods, like raw vegetables.

- Sterilise utensils and equipment for babies under 12 months.

- Check 'use by' dates, as food which has gone out of date can grow bacteria that cause illness. Throw away any food that looks or smells like it is going off.

- Always wash fresh fruit and vegetables; they might be carrying bacteria.

Personal hygiene

You can also spread bacteria if you do not follow good personal hygiene routines when making a feed or meal. You must:

- tie back long hair and wear a hair net if possible

- wear an apron and clean clothes; remove jewellery, such as rings

- use soap and warm water to wash your hands for at least 20 seconds; make sure you dry your hands thoroughly

- remember to wash your hands after touching raw meat/eggs, after going to the toilet or changing nappies, after touching bins or pets, after blowing your nose and after touching your face or hair

- keep your fingernails short and clean

- cover any wounds or cuts with a waterproof plaster – blue plasters are good as you will notice if they fall off and land in the food.

Environment

A clean and hygienic environment is important to help stop bacteria spreading. You can keep the area clean by wiping down surfaces, washing equipment in hot water and sterilising bottles.

Let's get practical!   8

Go on a learning walk in the food preparation area. Can you find these items?

- products for disinfecting surfaces, such as anti-bacterial spray

- detergents, such as washing up liquid, for washing equipment

- sterilising equipment for sterilising babies' bottles and feeding utensils

- hand soap and paper towels for washing and drying hands.

Over to you!   4

Explain what might happen to a baby or young child if feeds and meals are not prepared in a safe and hygienic environment.

3.4 How to evaluate planning and preparation of a feed/meal

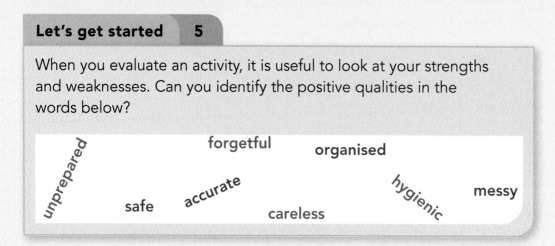
Do you ever stop to think about how things are going? Evaluating your own performance helps you to be able to do things better in the future.

Strengths/weaknesses

Think about how well you planned and carried out an activity, looking at your strengths and weaknesses.

You have looked at how to plan and prepare feeds and meals, and how to carry this out safely and hygienically. It is important to evaluate your own performance in planning and preparing a feed or meal.

Improvements/changes

Reflecting on your own performance will help you to identify where you can improve and what needs to be changed so that the activity goes better next time. Think about any difficulties you experienced and how these were overcome.

- Did you achieve what you set out to do?
- Did you forget anything?
- Could you have been more prepared?
- Were your timings correct?
- What would you do differently next time?

Case study

Penny's appraisal

Penny is the preschool cook. She plans the menus and makes the meals for the children.

Penny is preparing for her work appraisal. This is where she talks to her manager about how well she is working. She has been asked to think about her own strengths and weaknesses, relating to her job role. She notes down these thoughts:

Figure 2.31: Penny's work appraisal

Strengths (what I do well)

- I plan the correct portion sizes for the preschool children.
- I plan a balance of foods from the five food groups.
- I use equipment safely, using different coloured chopping boards.
- I always wash and dry my hands thoroughly.
- I keep the food preparation area hygienic by cleaning as I go.

Weaknesses (what I could do better)

- From time to time, I guess measurements, rather than weighing out ingredients.
- I sometimes forget to put my apron on straight away.
- Occasionally, I get confused with which colour cloth to use for washing up or wiping down surfaces.
- Sometimes I use a tea towel rather than oven gloves to take hot things out of the oven.

Check your understanding

1   Identify one strength and one weakness relating to Penny's personal hygiene.

2   Describe one thing that Penny could improve about the way she plans or prepares the meals.

3   Explain the benefits of Penny evaluating her own practice.

Review your learning

Test your knowledge   3

Read the statements. Two of them are FALSE. Identify and correct the false statements.

1 Evaluating your own performance only needs to be done before an appraisal.
2 Being honest about challenges can help you to overcome them in the future.
3 Talking about your weaknesses makes you a weak person.
4 Reflecting on areas for improvement can lead to positive changes.

What have you learnt?

	See section
• Current government dietary recommendations for healthy eating for children from birth to five years.	3.1
• Essential nutrients and their functions for children from birth to five years.	3.2
• Planning for preparing a feed/meal.	3.3
• How to evaluate planning and preparation of a feed/meal.	3.4

R059 Understand the development of a child from one to five years

Let's get started

How old do you think the children in the photo are? What does this photo tell you about their development? What can they do? What types of movements can they make?

What will you learn in this unit?

When working with young children in an early years setting it is important to understand how children develop and how this impacts on their play. You must also develop observation skills (watching and making notes) about children's development as this is the starting point for planning suitable play activities. Play helps children to move on in all areas of their development.

In this unit you will learn about:

- physical, intellectual and social developmental norms from one to five years **TA1**

- stages and types of play and how play benefits development **TA2**

- observe the development of a child aged one to five years **TA3**

- plan and evaluate play activities for a child aged one to five years for a chosen area of development **TA4**.

How you will be assessed

This unit will be assessed through a series of coursework tasks that show your understanding of each topic area. You will complete the assignment independently. The assignment will be marked by your teacher. The assignment contains two tasks, which will cover:

- completing an observation or observations of a child aged one to five years with teacher or adult supervision

- using findings to plan a suitable play activity for the child you observed and evaluating its success, strengths and weaknesses.

TA1

Physical, intellectual and social developmental norms from one to five years

Let's get started

What skills and abilities did you have by the time you started school?

Figure 3.1: Starting school

What will you learn?

- The expected development norms from one to five years.

1.1 The expected development norms from one to five years

Child development describes the sequence of changes that happen over time from birth to adulthood. Between one and five years old children develop new skills quickly. You might hear parents boast (show off) that their child is suddenly walking a few steps by themselves. As you develop your skills in observing children you will become familiar with what most children can do at each age and developmental stage. To understand the ways in which children develop it is helpful to break development into three separate areas: physical, intellectual and social.

Childcare experts observe large numbers of children to work out the average age at which children develop a particular ability or skill. They use this information to produce charts that show the developmental norms for each age group in each area of development. These **norms** are also referred to as **milestones**. Looking at norms or milestones helps parents and carers assess if a child is developing as expected. For example, should a two year old be able to feed themselves using a spoon? They are also used when planning activities to help children to reach their next milestones.

Physical development

Physical development describes how the different muscles in the body move and work together. There are two aspects of physical development (see Figure 3.2):

- **gross motor skills**
- **fine motor skills**.

Put your arm in the air. This is an example of a gross motor movement. Gross means 'large' in this case, rather than 'unpleasant'. Gross motor skills describes the control of the large muscles in the body including our arms, legs and trunk (body).

Now pick up a pen. This is an example of a fine motor movement. You are making a small, or fine, movement. Fine motor skills involve the control of the small muscles in our hands, fingers and toes.

Figure 3.2: Which child is using their gross motor skills? Which child is using their fine motor skills?

Let's get practical!   1

Do the following actions. For each activity state whether the movements involved gross motor skills or fine motor skills.

- Write your name.

- Run on the spot.

- Walk along a narrow line. Put out your arms if it helps you to keep your balance.

- Pick up a piece of scrunched-up paper with your toes.

Gross motor skills

By the time children reach one year old they already have many physical skills. Most children can crawl, stand and may have taken a few steps. These movements involve controlling the large muscles and maintaining balance. Children soon begin to walk and climb independently. By the time they start school they move with confidence, running, hopping and jumping. By this stage they will have developed the **coordination** needed for taking part in physical play. Table 3.1 gives some examples of gross motor skills and the ages at which most children develop these skills.

Table 3.1: Examples of gross motor skills

Age	Examples of gross motor skills
At one to two years	Stands holding on. Take their first steps at around 13 months but may lose balance and sit down suddenly.
By two years	Walks with confidence and runs. Climbs onto furniture. Can get on and propel a sit-on toy with their feet.
By three years	Hops. Can pedal a tricycle. Jumps on two feet. Can throw and kick a ball.
By four years	Stands on one leg and can tiptoe. Can balance to walk along a line. Climbs trees or on climbing frames.
By five years	Can run, dodge and skip. Throws or hits and catches a ball with aim. Can balance to walk along a low beam.

Fine motor skills

Children gradually develop the ability to coordinate the movement of the small muscles in their hands. A one-year-old child can pick up a small object using their first finger and thumb. This is called a **pincer grasp** (see Figure 3.3). At 18 months old a child can control their wrist to move an object such as a pencil, but will continue to hold it in their palm with their thumb and fingers wrapped around it. This is called a **palmer grasp** (see Figure 3.4).

Figure 3.3: Pincer grasp

By the age of three, a child will have developed greater control of their fingers so they can manage tricky tasks such as fastening shoes with Velcro straps, which helps them become independent. Table 3.2 gives some examples of fine motor skills and the ages at which most children develop these skills.

Figure 3.4: Palmer grasp

Table 3.2: Examples of fine motor skills

Age	Examples of fine motor skills
At one to two years	Holds objects in a palmer grasp. Picks up small objects using pincer grasp.
By 18 months	Can build a tower using three blocks. Drinks from a cup.
By two years	Can control a crayon, using a palmer grasp, to draw shapes. Turns pages of a book. Pulls on own shoes. Holds a spoon and helps to feed themselves.
By three years	Can control a pencil using thumb and fingers. Can thread large beads. Can build a tower with up to ten blocks. Can button and unbutton clothes. Uses a fork and spoon.
By four years	Can thread small beads. Draws figure and letter shapes. Uses scissors to cut out pictures. Can colour in shapes. Can dress themselves.
By five years	Can hold a pencil between their thumb and two fingers to write like an adult. Can thread a large needle and sew. Draws detailed pictures. Uses a knife and fork.

Case study

Maya

Maya is three and a half years old. She goes to a playgroup for two days each week. She is meeting the expected milestones for physical development. She loves to play outdoors and join in with drawing activities.

Check your understanding

1   Outline the difference between gross and fine motor skills development.

2   Explain how Maya's gross motor skills development can help her to take part in outdoor play.

3   Evaluate how Maya's fine motor skills development can support her independence.

Figure 3.5: Maya

Intellectual development

Intellectual development is the process by which children develop memory, and learn to think and solve problems. The first five years is an amazing time when children's minds are developing rapidly. Figure 3.6 shows different aspects of intellectual development.

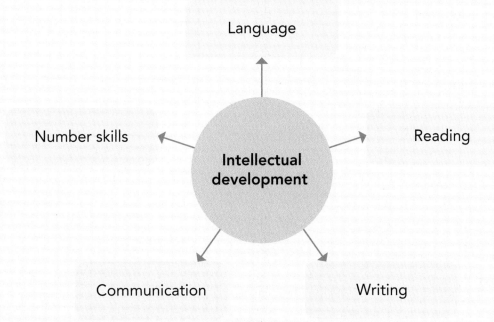

Figure 3.6: Aspects of intellectual development

Language

The sequence of language development is about how children learn to speak and listen. Language development is important for children to be able to express themselves and to respond when talking with other children and adults. It includes being able to make sounds and speak in words and sentences. Table 3.3 outlines the sequence of language developmental norms.

Table 3.3: The sequence of language developmental norms

Age	Norms of language development
Around one year old	Cries and responds with sounds. Begins to use familiar words such as 'dada' or 'dog'. Understands simple requests such as 'Give me the teddy'.
By 18 months	Knows and uses around 20 words.
Around two years old	May use around 50 words but understands far more. Listens and responds to simple instructions. Can link two to three words together such as 'me car' or 'look doggy'.
Around three years old	Uses around 300 words. Listens to others and asks questions. Uses simple sentences linking four to six words together but uses tenses incorrectly, for example 'goed to the park'.
Around four years old	Listens and responds to instructions and questions. Loves to chatter with adults and friends. Is beginning to use tenses correctly, for example 'I went to the park'. Uses joining words, for example 'I want to *because* Jamie's going'.
Around five years old	Grammar improves. Listens and pays full attention to adults. Asks relevant questions. Uses increasingly complex sentences.

Over to you!   1

a   Read the text below. State what age range you would expect Ajay and Tilly to be. They have both met their expected language norms.

> Ajay points and says the name of some things he knows such as 'cat' or 'car'. He can't put words he knows into a sentence yet but can understand what his friend means when she says, 'Give me the car'.

> Tilly is starting to speak in sentences, sometimes using up to six words. She often uses a word incorrectly, such as 'I sawed a doggy outside'.

b   Outline how Tilly's language skills are likely to change when she is one year older.

Reading

Reading and writing are about making sense of how written symbols (the letters of the alphabet) represent the sounds that form words. This is why sharing books from an early age is so important as it supports children's reading and writing development. When children become aware of words in books it encourages them to try to draw and write themselves. Most children learn to read and write formally when they start school at the age of four but their skills start to develop at a much earlier stage. Figure 3.7 shows how reading skills develop.

The early stage

The first stage, up to two years, is sometimes referred to as the pre-reading stage. Children are learning to enjoy books with an adult. They can turn pages and will point to pictures of things they recognise and name them.

Moving on

At around three to four years children have favourite books. They talk about the pictures and may even make up a story about them. They start to notice the printed letters and words and can point out common or familiar words.

Becoming a reader

At four to five years children enjoy books and can retell stories. They learn that the letters of the alphabet represent sounds (**phonics**). They begin to recognise some familiar words by their shape.

By five years old children can blend sounds to build words and read them, e.g. c-a-t, cat. They use these skills and the hints they get from looking at the pictures to read unfamiliar text.

Figure 3.7: How reading skills develop

Let's get practical!   2

Design a leaflet that gives advice to parents and carers of children aged one to two years. Include:

- a sentence that explains the importance of pre-reading skills for reading development
- three ways that parents and carers can help their child to enjoy looking at books.

Over to you!   2

1   Outline what is meant by pre-reading skills.

2   Explain why it helps children's reading development to point out and talk about the written words next to pictures.

3   Explain the skills needed for children to make sense of text in unfamiliar books.

Writing

Figure 3.8 explains how children's writing skills develop.

At around one to two years old children enjoy drawing. They may use crayons or paints to make random scribbles, lines or circles.

At two to three years old children can control pencils to produce simple drawings. They are aware of writing in books so 'pretend' letters of the alphabet begin to emerge in their drawings.

At around four years old children begin to string real letters together to form words. They often label their drawings and write their own name. They may not always spell words correctly and some letters may be reversed. They use the sounds they hear in speech to spell words such as 'snek' for 'snake'.

By five years old children begin to write for lots of different purposes such as lists, labels and cards. They can control a pencil well although their letters may not be evenly sized. They begin to write short sentences with spaces between words but may need help with spelling.

Figure 3.8: How writing skills develop

Let's get practical!   3

Produce a timeline that shows the stages of reading and writing.
This will help you when you observe children later in this unit.

Over to you!   3

1   State the age range of each of the following children. Each child has met their expected development norms.

   a   Sameer's favourite book is *Mr. Noisy* from the Mr. Men series. He likes to join in and say what's happening as his dad reads it. He points out the word and says 'noisy'. Sameer draws simple pictures but you can see letter shapes in his drawing.

   b   Molly enjoys reading and uses her knowledge of letter sounds to read words she doesn't know. She draws detailed pictures and can write a whole sentence.

   c   Bobby likes to share books with an adult. He points at the pictures and says the names of things he recognises. He uses a crayon to draw circles and lines.

2   Explain how sharing books can help children to develop their writing skills.

Communication

Communication is a two-way process. It is how we send and receive messages. You have already learnt how children communicate by using language to talk and to listen. Talking and listening are important skills but they are not the only ways in which children communicate with others (see Figure 3.9).

At one to two years old children have not developed their vocabulary (knowledge and use of words) enough to be able to explain how they feel or what they want but they can still communicate. If you watch a parent or carer with a one-year-old,

Figure 3.9: What does the way this child is sitting tell you about her feelings?

they communicate ('talk') to each other using **body language** such as smiles alongside verbal communication (sounds and words). At this age children cry if they are uncomfortable and chuckle if they are happy.

Although children over two years of age can speak and understand messages, communication is reinforced (made easier) by the use of body language.

One of the main ways we share messages is through our body language. Sometimes we use body language on its own but we almost always use it alongside sounds or speech. A parent may say 'no' to a child and at the same time shake their head to reinforce the message. Body language involves movements of the body such as:

- gestures (the movements we make with our hands or head to show meaning), for example nodding, pointing or thumbs up

- facial expressions, for example smiling, frowning or looking directly at another person (eye contact)

- large or whole-body movements, for example leaning forwards or folding our arms.

Children send messages using body language all the time. A one-year-old child will shake their head when they don't want any more food or point to something they do want. By three years of age children will lean forward and give eye contact if they are interested in a story. They might fold their arms if they are not happy about something.

Children understand the body language of others from an early age. For example, from one year old, a child knows they have done something well if an adult gives them the thumbs up sign and may smile back. If a two-year-old child was riding around on a wheeled toy and you held up your hand like a police officer they would stop. Watch a group of three to five year olds at play and you will see how they use body language to join in and build friendships.

Some children who have language difficulties use Makaton. This is a language programme that uses signs and symbols along with speech to help them develop their communication skills. It is based on the gestures used in British Sign Language (BSL). Makaton is used alongside speech to help children understand what is being said. For example, to use Makaton to say 'thank you', start with a flat hand with your fingertips on your chin. Move your hand down and away from you in an arc, while saying 'thank you'.

Over to you!   4

1   What do you think the following children are trying
to communicate?

   a   Sam, aged 18 months, points up at a toy car on top of
        the cupboard.

   b   Meena, aged two and a half, stamps her feet and folds
        her arms.

2   Suggest two ways you could give the message to a three year old
that you are pleased with their behaviour – without speaking!

Number skills

Let's get practical!   4

Young children start to develop number skills by joining in with
number rhymes. How many number rhymes can you think of?
Note them down.

By the time a child reaches the age of five they are already using thinking
and reasoning skills to come to terms with numbers. By this stage they
can count and add single-digit numbers. Number skills development
is a gradual process. Figure 3.10 shows the range of skills that a child
needs to develop; taking part in a range of games, number activities and
experiences will help them on their number journey.

At one to two years old children naturally sort objects when they play.
You may see a one-year-old child sitting their teddies together in a
group or putting objects into a box. This child is developing an early
understanding of sets of objects and by two years they will be able
to compare the groups and will know which group has more or fewer.
Children start to learn about number through games and rhymes.
They memorise number names to use when they count objects but may
say numbers out of order, for example 'one, four, two'.

At two to three years old, children start to use more advanced ways to
sort objects. It may be by colour, type of animal or ordering according
to size. They remember number names and will point to them when they
see them, for example on a front door or a bus. Children of this age
are beginning to recognise and point out similarities and differences in

pictures and by three years old can match them. They enjoy taking part in simple counting activities, touching each object in turn as they count. They may miss out numbers when counting, for example 'one, two, three, five, six'. Children of this age can hold up the correct number of fingers to show if you ask, 'How many?' (see Figure 3.11).

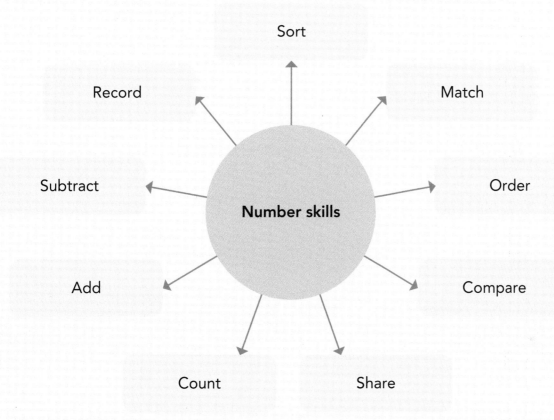

Figure 3.10: The number skills that children need to develop

At four years old children enjoy games involving numbers as they can count spots on a die and move a counter the correct number of spaces. They can match the correct numeral to a small number of objects in a set. They can record (write down) numerals although they may write them backwards. They use their numerical skills to share objects such as toys or sweets fairly between a small group.

Figure 3.11: Alex is showing you that she is three years old. At three years of age children can link number names (e.g. three) to numbers in a set (e.g. a set of three fingers).

By five years old most children have a good understanding of number. They are confident in counting up to 20 and sometimes more. They can recognise number patterns to count on in 2s, 5s or 10s and can count backwards from 10. They can solve simple number problems such as 'What is two more than three?', 'What is one less than five' or 'What is half of 4?'. Children can add and subtract objects up to 10 and record their answers.

Over to you!　5

1　Outline activities that help children aged two to develop their number skills.

2　Explain the difference in number development norms between children at one year old and three years old.

3　Evaluate how number games can help four to five year olds to develop their number skills.

Social development

Figure 3.12: What skills might these two-year-olds have that can help them to build a relationship with their early years educator and the other children?

Social development describes how children get to know others and interact with them. At first, a child builds relationships and connections with their parents and carers. Later on, they develop friendships with other children. Think about Figure 3.12. To develop socially, children learn a range of personal skills including:

- the ability to communicate with others

- acceptable behaviour

- sharing and taking turns

- becoming independent and growing **self-esteem**.

Communicating with others

Table 3.4 shows how children develop their communication skills.

Table 3.4: How children develop their communication skills

Age	How children communicate
At one to two years	Able to relate to parent or carer by listening and responding with body language, sounds and some spoken words.
At two to three years	Able to express feelings such as pleasure or distress. Can use language skills to help them to build relationships with parents and carers and make friendships with other children.
At three to four years	Will have two-way conversations with parents, carers and other children. Often have a special friend. Are becoming aware of others' feelings and will comfort someone who is upset.
At four to five years	Are less dependent on their parents. Are confident in communicating with a wider circle of friends and adults. Can suggest play ideas or negotiate in play with other children.

Acceptable behaviour

Behaviour is an outward sign of children's emotions (how they feel). Acceptable behaviour is about developing manners such as asking before taking something or saying 'please' and 'thank you'.

How a child behaves depends upon their stage of development. The age of the child must be considered when deciding if behaviour is acceptable or unacceptable. A one-year-old child might cry and throw themselves on the floor if they are upset and will just take something they want. This behaviour is expected from a one year old because they don't have the words to express themselves. If a four-year-old child behaved in the same way, this behaviour would be unacceptable. Table 3.5 shows the developmental norms of acceptable behaviour in children.

Table 3.5: How children develop manners

Age group	Behaviour norms
At one year of age	Children are unaware of what is acceptable behaviour and don't realise the effect of their behaviour on others.
By 18 months	Children are unable to control their behaviour and often have tantrums if upset.
	They understand what 'no' means but may need to be reminded.
At two to three years	Children can use words to say how they feel but at times still find it difficult to control their temper.
	By three years they are more aware of what behaviour is acceptable.
	They are developing good manners and will often ask before taking something and say 'please' or 'thank you' if reminded.
At three to four years	Children know right from wrong.
	They may sometimes show unacceptable behaviour to get attention.
	They want approval from parents or carers and often seek praise by saying things such as 'Am I a good boy?'.
	They remember to say please and thank you.
At four to five years	Children understand what acceptable behaviour in different situations is, such as having good manners at mealtimes.
	They may still have difficulty in controlling their anger at times but understand that it is unacceptable.
	By five years old, children realise the effect their behaviour might have.
	They show thoughtfulness and use kind words to others because they want to be liked.

Sharing

Being able to share and take turns are difficult skills for children to develop.

At one to two years old, children want attention from their parents or carers quickly so they can't wait or take turns. They are possessive (selfish) with toys and may snatch toys from other children. It is important to understand that this is usual behaviour at this age. These children are not being naughty. They have not yet mastered the skills needed to wait and share. Children continue to be possessive with toys until they are around three years old.

From three years old, children are more willing to share but only for a short time. They can now take turns but will still need help from an adult.

For example, they will understand and be patient if an adult tells them it's their turn next for the bike but they still need an adult to organise turns.

By four to five years old, children can play games where they take turns. They understand and can agree to rules in games and will even remind others of the rules.

Independence/self-esteem

At one to two years old, children are almost totally dependent on their parent or carer. At this age they do not see themselves as separate and independent individuals so have not yet developed their **self-image** (sense of who they are). At two to three years old they start to have an awareness their own self-image and are becoming independent. They are happy to leave their parent or carer for a short period of time.

Self-image influences children's self-esteem. Self-esteem develops as a result of how children see themselves. By the age of three to four, children are more confident and have clear likes and dislikes. They can make choices and play independently. They are able to do things for themselves such as dressing or feeding themselves.

At four to five years old children become more aware of their own skills and abilities and compare themselves with their friends. This usually builds self-esteem but if their skills are delayed it could have a negative impact.

Let's get practical!   5

Design a simple game or activity for a two year old that will encourage sharing.

Make a list of games for three to five year olds that encourage turn taking.

Stretch

You work in an early years setting in the toddler room caring for children aged one to two years. One of the parents is concerned about the development of their child, aged 18 months. Produce an advice leaflet for the parent, giving a detailed explanation of the physical, intellectual and social development norms they should expect.

Holistic development

Holistic development means how a child is developing as a whole person. It includes their physical, intellectual and social development. Although it is helpful to learn about each area of development separately it is important to remember that they are all happening at the same time. For example, at around 15 months a child walks without help and at the same time is learning new words and developing clear likes and dislikes.

It is also important to consider how the three areas of development are interrelated (dependent on each other). Making progress in one area can support the progress in others. For example, if a child has good physical skills, it helps them to join in outdoor play and build friendships with other children. Fine motor skills are needed to be able to develop writing skills.

Over to you!   6

1   Note one development norm for physical development, intellectual development and social development for a three-year-old child.

2   Explain how communication skills might impact on the behaviour of a child aged two years.

Sequence of development

You have learnt about the norms for each area of development. These norms are always in the same order and all children will reach the milestones in the same order, although not always at the same age. For example, they cannot speak a sentence before they have learnt the words they need.

Children are unique

Although children follow the same developmental sequence it is important to remember that every child is unique. They move along the development pathway at their own pace. Childcare experts base development norms on what most children can do at a certain age. It is not surprising then that some children develop at a slower pace and some faster. For example, most children take their first steps at around 13 months, but some not until they are 15 months or even later.

Why children may develop differently

It is important to observe children's progress to check if they are developing as expected. You will learn more about how to observe children in Section 3.1. If development is delayed, it could mean a child needs help to develop certain skills. Children may have a delay in all development areas or in one or two areas.

Developmental delay could be related one or more of the following reasons:

- the environment (access to space and resources)
- speech and language difficulties
- a physical disability
- a learning disability.

Children need to be provided with the right environment. A lack of opportunity to play outdoors can lead to a delay in developing physical skills and making friends. A lack of opportunity to share books can impact on developing communication skills.

Speech and language difficulties affect how children communicate. This can lead to delays in making friends as well as in developing reading and writing skills.

Development can be delayed by a physical disability (for example, gross motor difficulties that affect the muscles and the coordination of movement). A physical disability may prevent children joining in physical play with others, impacting on building friendships.

A learning disability can impact on speech and language development and writing skills. A child's thinking skills and problem-solving skills can also be affected. They may have difficulty in taking part in puzzle activities or number games where they need to count.

Over to you!   7

Use what you have learnt about development norms in this chapter to:

a   Explain the relationship between self-esteem and independence.

b   Evaluate the importance of understanding whether or not a child has a delay in an area of their development.

Review your learning

Test your knowledge

1 Explain how childcare experts decide on the norms for each age group.

2 Explain why charts that describe norms (milestones) are important for parents and carers.

3 Outline the meaning of each of the three areas of development.

4 Describe what is meant by development norms.

5 Outline why using number rhymes with children from one to two years is important for their number development.

6 Explain the development of counting skills from children aged two to five years.

7 Discuss how intellectual skills are used to solve number problems.

What have you learnt?

	See section
• The expected development norms from one to five years.	1.1

Stages and types of play and how play benefits development

Let's get started 1

What type of play do you think these children are involved in?

How is their stage of development helping them to join in with this play?

Figure 3.13: Play benefits development.

What will you learn?

- The stages of play.
- The types of play.
- How play benefits development.

2.1 The stages of play

If you watch children at play, it might appear that they are just having fun, but it is much more than that. Their stage of play not only impacts on the way they play but also helps them to reach the next stage of development. Children enjoy lots of different types of play but let's first look at how their play develops.

Solitary

The early stage of play up to two years of age is called **solitary play**. If you watch one year olds at play, you will see how they are totally engrossed in handling toys and exploring everything they find in the environment around them. Through their play they learn about their own bodies and what they can do. Although there may be other children in the room they don't take any notice of them. However, children of this age still like to be near to a parent or carer.

Examples of solitary play include:

- playing with toy cars, for example running them along the floor and saying 'brrrr', then banging them together
- taking objects out of and then putting them back into a basket
- banging on pots and pans with a wooden spoon.

Parallel

At around two to three years of age children play alongside but not with other children – this is known as **parallel play**. At this stage they are becoming more aware of what other children are doing. Seeing another child enjoying their play makes them want to copy it. Children sometimes choose the same kind of toy or resource but they are still possessive of their own things. You may see a child playing next to others to:

- make their own dough model – they may share moulds and cutters
- complete their own puzzle sitting next to others doing the same
- build their own sandcastles in a sand box alongside another child.

Associate

Associate play (also known as associative play) happens at around three to four years old. It helps children start to build friendships. They often say what they are doing and may share or swap toys. Children sometimes join in the same activity but they are not really playing together. This type of play has no clear plan. Children don't discuss what's happening with each other but play in their own way. They don't really follow the same ideas or rules about the play.

Examples include:

- riding around with others on wheeled toys or scooters – they may go in the same direction and do the same actions but they don't discuss it

- joining in building with blocks but without making plans about what is being built or talking about their own role in the construction.

Cooperative

Cooperative play happens at around four to five years when children are making firm friendships. This stage of play relies on:

- good communication

- sharing

- taking turns.

Children think about what to play, and agree on the rules and the goals (what they want the outcome to be) of the play. As they play, they talk about how their play is progressing and may even suggest new ideas such as resources they could use. There may be disagreements along the way but children often use their negotiation skills to sort out problems without involving an adult.

Examples include:

- playing 'house', with each child playing the role of a member of a family

- playing a ball game where they've agreed turns and how to score

- deciding what model to build and discussing which materials to use, then each child taking part in making it.

Test your knowledge   1

1. List the stages of play and link them to the expected age groups.
2. Explain the difference between associate and cooperative play.
3. Evaluate the importance of communication for cooperative play.

2.2 The types of play

Let's get started   2

One type of play children enjoy is imaginative play where they pretend to be characters and act out stories. How many more types of play can you think of?

The UK guidance for the Early Years Foundation Stage (EYFS) stresses the importance of play for children to develop and learn new skills. There are many types of play that can help children's development.

Figure 3.14 shows the different types of play you will explore.

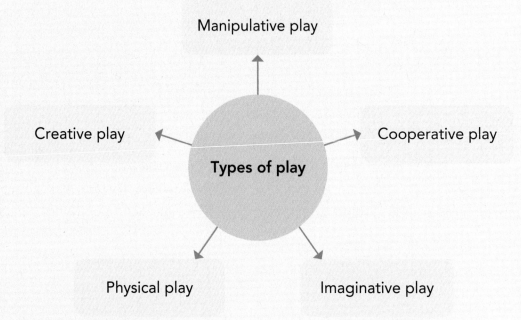

Figure 3.14: Types of play

You may notice children using more than one type of play at the same time. For example, a childcare worker may decide to set out puzzles to develop children's manipulative skills. If two children decide to complete a puzzle together, it would also be cooperative play.

Manipulative play

'Manipulate' means to handle and control something. In **manipulative play** children use their fine motor skills to move, turn and explore objects and toys. It can involve putting things together or taking them apart. The resources and materials children use in manipulative play are dependent upon their fine motor skills. For example, a four year old would enjoy threading small beads but this **play activity** would be frustrating for a one year old because they haven't yet developed fine motor movements in their fingers. A one year old would enjoy holding a toy in their palm and turning and exploring it. Remember that children may use pincer and palmer grasps to pick up and hold objects until they are around three years old (see Topic Area 1, Section 1.1).

Table 3.6 shows examples of manipulative play where children use fine motor skills.

Table 3.6: Examples of manipulative play where children use their fine motor skills

Manipulative play	Skills by age	Materials and resources
Exploring toys and materials	At around one year old, children use their hands and fingers to hold and manipulate objects.	Rattles, wooden spoons, hairbrushes
	By two years of age, they enjoy finding out how things move, for example pulling, turning and pushing. Also putting things in and getting them out of boxes.	Toy vehicles Natural materials such as fir cones Dolls and teddies with clothes to fasten and unfasten
Puzzles	At one to two years children can slot things into a space.	Shape-sorting puzzles (posting boxes)
	At two to three years old they like fitting things together and taking them apart.	Puzzles with slot-in shapes
	From three years, children enjoy fitting together puzzle pieces to make a picture.	Table-top and floor puzzles
Drawing and painting	At one to two years old, children enjoy mark-making (scribbles) and hand printing.	Chunky crayons, paint
	From two years they like drawing, painting, and finger painting.	Chunky crayons, felt-tip pens, paint brushes, sponges, printing blocks
	From three years old they like block and potato printing, painting and chalk drawing.	Felt-tip pens, chalks, paint brushes, sponges, printing blocks, rollers, easels
	From four years old children enjoy using their fingers to control a computer mouse or use a touch screen.	Computers and drawing programs

Table 3.6: Continued

Manipulative play	Skills by age	Materials and resources
Construction play	From one year they enjoy stacking objects.	Stacking beakers or rings
	From two years they enjoy building with blocks.	Wooden building blocks
	From three to four years they enjoy building models using interlocking construction pieces.	Toy construction bricks
Modelling	From two years old they can use their fingers to roll, flatten and change the shape of materials.	Clay, play dough

Let's get practical!   1

Test out your own manipulative skills. For example, depending on the resources you have, you could:

- do a puzzle with small pieces
- use modelling materials
- thread a needle and sew
- draw an intricate picture.

Think about the skills you used. How did you hold the materials or implements? How did you move and manipulate them? How did you use your hands? Did you need to use all your fingers?

Test out holding things or picking them up using a palmer grasp and a pincer grasp. Do you need to use more fingers to hold things more securely?

Cooperative play

Cooperative play happens when two or more children play together for an agreed purpose such as playing board games or lotto with rules or ball games with scoring.

The main features of cooperative play are:

- **Social interaction:** social interaction is essential in cooperative play. For example, children need to talk and agree which game to play, how to play the game, who does what, and who goes first and why.

- **Agreeing goals:** goals are the things children want to achieve through their play. Goals may be agreed before or during the play. Children then work together cooperatively to make sure that the goals are met.

For example, how they will score when throwing beanbags at a target or what needs to happen to win the game.

- **Play with rules:** the rules of play are the guidelines that have to be followed. Play often has specific rules to follow in board games. In cooperative play, children agree and keep to the rules of play. Children often remind each other of the rules and may negotiate a change in rules during play.

- **Child led:** during cooperative play, it is the children who decide what to play, what their goals are, and how the play develops. For example, they might decide to use a set of picture lotto cards in a different way. They might suggest a different way to play a game, such as 'Shall we go down ladders and up snakes?' in a game of snakes and ladders. An adult may help children to take turns in board games. They may encourage a certain type of play by providing resources and materials for a project or game but they do not to tell the children how they should play or what the goals should be.

Case study

Greenhill School

At Greenhill School the teacher wants to encourage cooperative play among a group of three four years olds. He puts out lots of junk materials including cardboard tubes, boxes, plastic bottles and wooden sticks.

One of the children soon suggests building a 'robot tank'. They begin working together, discussing what to use and what the tank should look like. They agree it should have wheels with spikes sticking out. They sort the materials and start to build their tank, making suggestions for alternative ways to build it or other materials to use.

Figure 3.15: Cooperative play

Check your understanding

1. Outline the ways the teacher is supporting cooperative play.

2. Explain the importance of this group project for these four-year-old children.

3. Explain the skills these children will need to be able to take part in cooperative play.

Imaginative play

Imaginative play is sometimes called 'make-believe' play. It happens when children act out their ideas. They may role play everyday situations with friends such as shopping or being at the hospital. Children may take on roles that reflect experiences they have had such as travelling on a bus, going to the zoo or the seaside. Sometimes they play out imaginative experiences such as travelling into space. Table 3.7 explains types of imaginative play.

Table 3.7: Types of imaginative play

Type of imaginative play	How children play	Resources
Role play	Children pretend to be a person in a work or domestic setting such as a parent, shopkeeper or doctor. You may see this type of play starting at two to three years old, for example a child pours cups of 'pretend' tea. Older children develop their play using a range of props to make it more lifelike.	Home corner: props such as tables, crockery, saucepans Supermarket: props such as empty food boxes, bags, money, till, telephone GP surgery: props such as bed, doctor's/nurse's uniform, stethoscope, bandages
Puppet play	From around the age of one, children enjoy puppet play. By the age of three they use puppets to act out a story. At four years they may follow a story created on a story board.	Hand puppets Finger puppets Puppet theatres
Dramatic play/ acting	At around three years of age, children dress up and can be anyone from their imagination. They could be deep sea explorers or astronauts. They may have watched films and become superheroes.	Dressing-up clothes, for example hats and helmets, shoes, masks, capes Pieces of fabric
Small world play	From about three years of age, children use small figures, moving them around to retell stories they know or they make up stories from their imagination.	Play people Toy vehicles, such as cars, trains and train tracks Toy animals and dinosaurs Dolls house
Story board	A story board is a sequence of pictures that tell a story. They show children what happens first, how the story moves on and what happens at the end. From around three years of age, children follow the sequence of the story and use their imagination to create the storyline in their play. They might use resources or act out the story themselves.	Puppets Small world figures

Physical play

Physical play is any kind of play that helps children to develop their gross motor skills (see Section 1.1). It involves movements such as climbing, running, kicking or throwing. Children need space for physical play so it often, but not always, takes place outdoors. Figure 3.16 shows various types of physical play and the resources that can be used to support them.

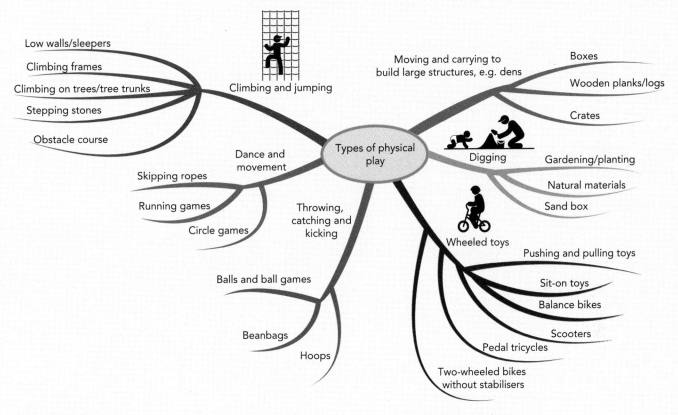

Figure 3.16: Types of physical play and the resources that can be used to support them

Let's get practical!   2

Produce a planning sheet for one week for a group of two year olds who attend a play group. For each day, suggest one physical (gross motor) and one manipulative (fine motor) play activity. Try to include activities that use different types of resources for each day.

Creative play

Creative play allows children to use their imagination to express their ideas. How children express themselves depends upon their stage of development (see Topic Area 1, Section 1.1). A one- or two-year-old child will enjoy finger painting whilst a three-year-old child may paint a recognisable picture. The outcome of creative play could be an artefact (a product you can touch) such as a model or it could be the creation of sounds or movements. If children are shown a picture to copy or told which movements to make, they are not being creative in their play because they are not expressing their own ideas.

Table 3.8 shows examples of creative play and the resources and materials that can support it.

Table 3.8: Examples of creative play and resources and materials that can support it

Type of creative play	How children play	Useful resources and materials
Art: mark-making, drawing and painting	Finger, hand painting and printing Drawing and painting pictures, chalking on ground and walls Creative computer programmes	Paints, chalks, crayons, felt-tips Computers and programmes
Modelling	Making an artefact from waste materials in junk modelling Moulding materials into shapes Puppet making	Cardboard boxes and tubes Tape, glue Paint Play dough, clay Fabric
Collage	Creating pictures using different materials Decorating objects such as boxes	Natural materials such as leaves or stones, shells Fabric, buttons, ribbon Paper, tissue Glue
Music and dance	Singing games Using musical instruments or objects to explore sounds or beating time to music Responding (moving) to music	Percussion instruments such as shakers, bells, drums Everyday objects such as tin cans, saucepans and spoons CDs

Over to you! 1

Give examples of resources that could encourage children to:

a produce a collage

b take part in role play

c make music/sounds.

Test your knowledge 2

1 Give two examples of play activities for each type of play: manipulative, cooperative, imaginative, physical and creative.

2 Give two examples of role-play settings suitable for children aged three to five years. Suggest resources that can be used.

3 Explain the difference between role play and dramatic play/acting.

4 Evaluate the role of language skills in imaginative play.

2.3 How play benefits development

Let's get started 3

What types of play are shown in the photo? What are the benefits of these types of play for children's development?

Figure 3.17: Play is the main way that children develop their physical, intellectual, social and creative skills.

Physical development

Figure 3.18 summarises the skills children need for physical development.

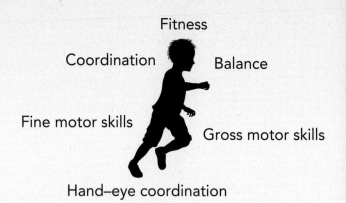

Figure 3.18: Skills for physical development

Children need regular opportunities to take part in physical play activities to develop their gross motor skills (see Topic Area 1, Section 1.1). By the time they are one year old most children can reach, crawl or roll towards toys, which helps them to strengthen their arms and learn to coordinate their movements. Pulling themselves up to stand or using push-a-long toys strengthens their leg muscles. By the time children are more active at two years of age, any activity that involves climbing, kicking, riding or throwing and catching helps fitness, strengthens muscles and improves coordination.

Many manipulative play activities help children to improve their fine motor skills (see Topic Area 1, Section 1.1) for example by:

- threading and sewing

- colouring, drawing and writing

- throwing and catching

- fastening and buttoning clothes on dolls or dressing-up clothes.

Some activities, such as when children mould, twist and flatten play dough, help to strengthen their fingers and hands.

Manipulative play is also beneficial as it helps to develop children's **hand–eye coordination**. Imagine threading a needle and think about how you are using your eyes and fingers together. This is an example of hand–eye coordination. It means using the eyes to guide the hands to carry out a movement or task. As well as helping children in their play, hand–eye coordination is essential for independent activities such as feeding and dressing themselves.

Balance and coordination are important aspects of a child's physical development. Balance means being able to control the body when moving and when still. You may have seen a one-year-old fall onto their bottom when they first start to walk. That's because they haven't yet developed the balance and coordination of their limbs. Play where children must adjust and coordinate their movements helps to improve balance and coordination.

Activities to support balance and coordination includes:

- **wheeled toys:** baby walkers, scooters, balance bikes, tricycles
- **climbing:** on frames, trees and logs
- crossing low beams, stepping stones.

Fitness for children means having the strength and stamina (staying power) to carry out activities involving running, climbing or jumping. Any play that involves movement and exercise contributes to strengthening children's muscles and bones and promoting healthy hearts and lungs.

Intellectual development

Through play children make sense of their world and develop intellectually. They need opportunities to explore things around them, find out how things work, make decisions and communicate their thoughts. Figure 3.19 shows aspects of intellectual development that are enhanced through play.

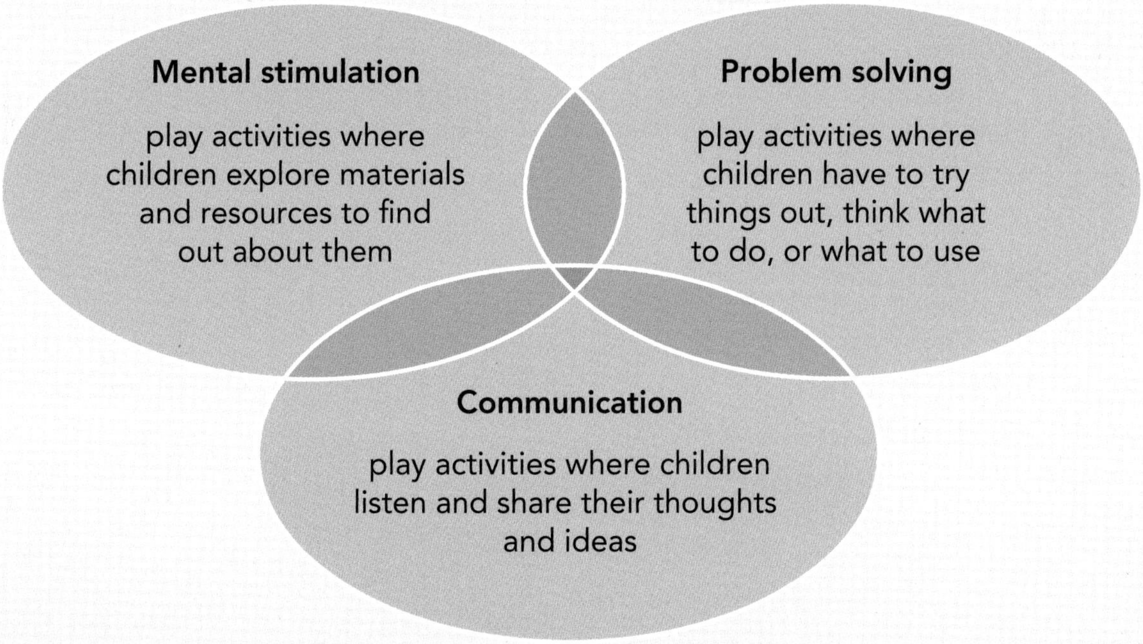

Mental stimulation

play activities where children explore materials and resources to find out about them

Problem solving

play activities where children have to try things out, think what to do, or what to use

Communication

play activities where children listen and share their thoughts and ideas

Figure 3.19: Intellectual development through play

Different types of activities can help to promote intellectual development. Games, including technology games and puzzles, are particularly helpful. Children have to use strategy (think about their approach to a problem) as they play. Problem solving is about learning through trial and error (testing things out). If a piece doesn't fit, or pressing a button doesn't work, children need to rethink and try something else.

Games and puzzles promote:

- **Mental stimulation:** children have to make decisions about how to play a game, and think about and use rules. Simple technological toys may require children to think about what happens when they click on something or press a button.

- **Problem solving skills:** in puzzle play children must use their knowledge to think about which puzzle piece or shape might fit. In dice games they may need to think through a strategy, for example 'What happens if I throw a six?', 'What number do I have to get to win?'

- **Communication:** children are encouraged to ask questions and talk to adults and other children as they work to solve problems.

When children take part in creative play they also use and develop their intellectual skills. For example, creative play gives them the opportunity to think about and make choices. They must think about what's happening when they handle and use different resources and materials.

Creative play promotes:

- mental stimulation, for example when mixing paint colours together and discovering a new colour

- problem solving, for example, what to do if the glue doesn't stick the items together in the way they expected it to

- communication skills by talking about their ideas, showing their pictures and learning new words.

Children are always excited when exploring the natural world. This excitement will prompt them to ask questions, investigate and think about the world around them. Natural world play involves activities such as water, sand or growing things. It gives children the opportunity to investigate how materials change and react.

Natural world play encourages:

- mental stimulation as children discover how things change or react in different situations – for example, what leaves feel like in autumn or what happens if they blow through a straw into water

- problem solving, for example 'Is wet or dry sand best for building castles?' or 'What do plants need to grow?'

- **communication:** because children get excited about their discoveries and are keen to talk about what they are doing as they learn new words.

Children love to share stories and rhymes with adults and other children. In storytelling activities, children's minds are stimulated if they are asked to point out pictures or words. A one year old may learn their first words through games such as pat-a-cake or nursery rhymes. When looking at books, children have to concentrate and think about what's happening.

Sharing stories and rhymes encourages:

- **mental stimulation:** when children learn and join in with rhymes or songs it improves their memory and recall

- **communication skills:** children talk about pictures, what's happening in the story and what might happen next, and learn new words.

Over to you!   2

A parent of a three-year-old has asked for advice from nursery staff on play ideas that will benefit his child's intellectual development.

a   Outline three play activities that would be beneficial. Think about the child's stage of development.

b   For each activity explain how it can stimulate the child's problem-solving skills.

c   Evaluate the extent to which each play activity is likely to promote communication skills.

Social skills

Play helps children to develop the social skills they need for life such as independence, confidence and self-esteem.

At one to two years of age, children's social development is very much dependent on play that is led by their parent or carer. Play helps them to build relationships and encourages communication. Playing simple games such as rolling a ball back and forth develops an understanding of sharing and turn taking. Joining in with rhymes, songs or a game of 'peek-a-boo' (where the adult hides their face with their hands, and then suddenly takes away their hands and says 'Peek-a-boo!') is great fun and helps children to build an awareness of what they can do. This helps them to develop confidence and self-esteem.

At two years old, children enjoy playing alongside other children (see 'Parallel play' in Topic Area 2, Section 2.1). They enjoy drawing, craft and sand play, and are starting to share resources. Children gain confidence by copying other children because they learn new skills which help them to do things independently. Many play activities that this age group enjoy promote self-help skills. For example, they love tea-party play (setting a table and pouring 'pretend tea' into cups) or dressing dolls.

Activities supported by an adult, for example planting seeds or helping to make cookies, promote communication skills. The adult can ask and answer questions and introduce new vocabulary. These types of activity encourage children to become independent and boost their self-esteem.

Between three and five years old, children are ready to build friendships so play with other children is essential to their development. When children are in control of their play it builds their self-esteem because they feel good about themselves. It increases their confidence to test out their skills.

Over to you!   **3**

a   Research three rhymes that could be enjoyed by children aged one to two years old.

b   Explain how copying other children's play can promote confidence and independence.

Imaginative play, such as role play, allows children to follow their own interests. In role play children have to adapt their behaviour and learn to compromise (to give and take) and sort out disagreements. This needs more advanced skills in communication. Role play often involves dressing up, which helps develop self-care skills leading to greater independence.

Through group play, children of this age learn how to communicate, work together, plan and share. Group projects involve working together to produce something. Group projects include:

- construction activities

- building a train track

- art projects such as collage or junk modelling

- cooking.

In group projects, children have to take turns with tools and resources, which helps to promote sharing and self-control. They learn that by working together and sharing they can achieve their goals. Working with others helps children to practise and develop new skills, leading to increased independence. A finished project means that children feel good about their achievements – boosting their confidence and self-esteem.

Over to you!   4

These children are part of a group doing a project. Explain how this cooking activity might benefit their:

1   independence

2   confidence and self-esteem

3   sharing skills.

Figure 3.20: Cooking activity

Creative skills

Creative development is about how children learn to use their imagination to explore their ideas and respond to experiences. In activities that benefit creativity, children produce something or express themselves. This could be through making something, by their movements or by making sounds. It's important that children have the opportunity to explore their ideas, make decisions and solve problems through play.

Over to you!   5

a   Outline a creative activity appropriate for a three year old.

b   Give an example of how your activity can benefit the child's:

    i   fine motor development

    ii   social skills

    iii   creative skills.

Stretch

Joni, Sarah and Abdul are playing shop. It's one of their favourite activities. They play the roles of shopkeeper or customers, display things to sell, use a toy till and money, and make shopping lists.

Evaluate the benefits to development of shop role play. You should refer to physical and intellectual development and social and creative skills in your answer.

Review your learning

Test your knowledge   3

1   Describe activities that promote hand–eye coordination.

2   Explain how ride-on wheeled toys can help balance and coordination.

3   Evaluate the benefits of outdoor play and exercise for improved fitness.

4   Discuss the benefits of working as part of a group project for childrens' social skills.

What have you learnt?

	See section
• The stages of play.	2.1
• The types of play.	2.2
• How play benefits development.	2.3

Observe the development of a child aged one to five years

Let's get started

If you are working with children, observation (watching and listening to children to find out about their skills, abilities, interests and how they play) is an essential part of your role.

What do you think you can learn about a child by watching them play?

What will you learn?

- Observation and recording.

3.1 Observation and recording

Methods of observation

Observations are used for three main reasons:

- To find out whether a child is meeting their expected development norms. Observing a child will give you information about how they are developing physically, intellectually and socially (see Topic Area 1, Section 1.1). If a child's development is delayed in any area, plans can be put into place to support them to progress.

- To understand a child's stage of play and find out what they enjoy doing. An observation will tell you how a child is developing in terms of how they play and allow you to compare your findings with the expected stage of play for each age group (see Topic Area 2, Section 2.1). For example, are they able to share and play with other children? Are they able to cooperate? If they are not meeting the expected stage of play, the child can be supported to help them move towards it.

- To find out what type of play the child likes to be involved in and what they enjoy doing. This will depend upon their age, interests and temperament. For example, do they enjoy physical outdoor play, or do they prefer to sit quietly and make things?

It is helpful to see observation as part of a cycle. See Figure 3.21.

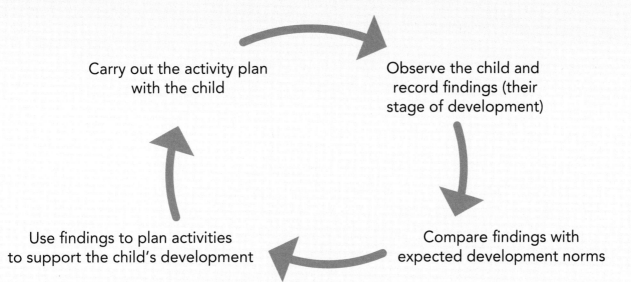

Carry out the activity plan with the child

Observe the child and record findings (their stage of development)

Use findings to plan activities to support the child's development

Compare findings with expected development norms

Figure 3.21: How observations are used as part of a cycle of observation and planning

The observation method you choose will depend on what you want to find out about a child. You may want to know whether they have achieved a particular skill, such as whether or not they can catch a ball, or whether they are able to take turns when playing a game.

Four methods of observation used by early years educators are:

- narrative
- checklist
- snapshot
- time sample.

See Table 3.9 for an overview of these methods.

Table 3.9: An overview of the four methods of observation

Method of observation	What the method involves
Narrative	A detailed written description of what is being observed over a short period of time.
Checklist	A list of possible skills is produced so that the observer can check off the child's skills as they are observed.
Snapshot	A brief note is made about a child to capture something they do or a skill they use.
Time sample	Capturing information about what a child is doing at particular times of the day. It could be how they play or how they behave.

Narrative observations

Write a short account (taking no more than one minute) of your journey to school or to the shops or the bus stop.

Read it through. Was it difficult to explain? Is your account clear?

A narrative is a written description or account of something. A narrative observation is a detailed running record of what a child is doing or saying over a short period of time, usually no more than a few minutes. It can be written on a notepad or in the child's ongoing development record without much preparation. A **narrative observation** is appropriate for capturing evidence about a child's holistic development as it captures everything the child is doing. For example, you could use this method to answer questions such as: Is the child playing alongside or with others? What are they saying? What physical skills are they using?

Table 3.10 shows the advantages and disadvantages of the narrative method of observation.

Table 3.10: Advantages and disadvantages of a narrative observation

Advantages	Disadvantages
Can observe any aspect of a child's development. Gives a good picture of the child's overall development. If there is a pen and a piece of paper handy, it can be done without preparation when the child is doing something of interest.	It's impossible to write down everything the child is doing or saying. The observer could give an opinion rather than writing a factual account (being **subjective**). It can be difficult to come up with appropriate descriptive terms on the spur of the moment.

As the observer, you need a pen and a piece of paper, notepad or printed template on which to produce a clearly written running record of what you see. It is important that the record is an **objective** description of what is seen. It's helpful to add comments shortly after the observation whilst it is fresh in the memory.

Figure 3.22 shows an example of a narrative observation record.

OBSERVATION FORM

Name:	Age:
Observer:	Date / time:

Record of observation	Comments

Include the name (first name or initials for confidentiality) and age of the child, the name of the observer, the date and time the observation was completed.

Only write down what you see – don't try to interpret it. For example, don't add: 'He is interested in what they are doing'.

Use the present tense. For example, use 'goes' not 'went'.

Use child's initials to help you write quickly.

Figure 3.22: Example of a narrative observation record

Over to you!   1

Narrative observations must be objective. Read these example phrases from a narrative observation.

1. For each statement identify if they are objective or subjective.

   a   J is very angry with P.

   b   D uses a pincer grasp to pick up the small bead.

   c   N pushes L with his right hand.

   d   S is enjoying playing with the train track.

2. Rewrite those you identify as subjective.

Checklist observations

A checklist (sometimes called a tick list) is the method most appropriate for observing specific skills. It is a list of statements, such as 'Can walk without help', or 'Can count to ten'. It has to be prepared before the observation takes place but once prepared it is easy to use. The observer watches to see whether the child can use a particular skill and if they can, the observer puts a tick against the appropriate statement.

Table 3.11 shows the advantages and disadvantages of a **checklist observation**.

Table 3.11: Advantages and disadvantages of an observation checklist

Advantages	Disadvantages
It can be targeted to a particular child and to specific skills.	It doesn't give any detail – it only shows whether a child has or hasn't developed a skill unless comments are added.
It's easy to use as there is no need to write during the observation. Comments can be added later to clarify information.	The child may choose not to show their skill when the observer is watching.
It's an easy way to check a child's progress against expected norms.	It doesn't give information on how confident the child is in using a skill or how often they use it.

To conduct and record a checklist observation, you will need a prepared list of what you want to learn about the child. It is important that it records what the child can do. If the child hasn't achieved a skill yet, the tick box should be left unchecked. This is because the child may be able to achieve the skill soon or they may not have shown it at the time of the observation. It is helpful to have a space for comments that can be added later.

Figure 3.23 shows an example of a checklist observation record.

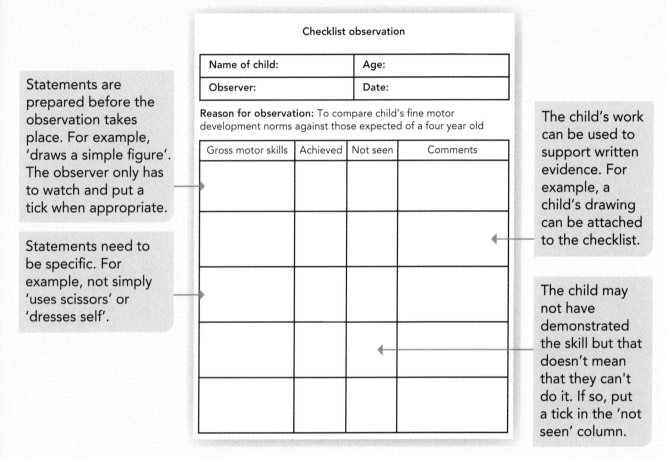

Statements are prepared before the observation takes place. For example, 'draws a simple figure'. The observer only has to watch and put a tick when appropriate.

Statements need to be specific. For example, not simply 'uses scissors' or 'dresses self'.

The child's work can be used to support written evidence. For example, a child's drawing can be attached to the checklist.

The child may not have demonstrated the skill but that doesn't mean that they can't do it. If so, put a tick in the 'not seen' column.

Checklist observation

| Name of child: | | Age: | |
| Observer: | | Date: | |

Reason for observation: To compare child's fine motor development norms against those expected of a four year old

Gross motor skills	Achieved	Not seen	Comments

Figure 3.23: Example of a checklist observation record

Let's get practical!   2

Design a checklist to find out if a two-year-old child has achieved their expected gross motor development norms.

Snapshot observations

A **snapshot observation** shows what a child is doing or saying in a brief moment in time. It is usually unplanned. It is a very quick, short written record made by an adult when a child is seen doing something interesting or demonstrating a particular new skill. For example, it could be when they take their first step or link two words together for the first time. Early years professionals often have sticky notes handy for this purpose. Snapshot observations contribute to the ongoing assessment of a child's development.

Table 3.12 shows the advantages and disadvantages of this method of observation.

Table 3.12: Advantages and disadvantages of a snapshot observation

Advantages	Disadvantages
Doesn't need to be planned ahead.	Gives little detail.
Provides evidence of a new skill that a child has developed.	May be written down on a small piece of notepaper that can easily be lost or not filed away securely.
Contributes evidence to other methods of observation.	May be a subjective record.

Sticky notes should be filed away safely with the child's personal information to protect the child's privacy.

Often sticky notes are used but this information could be recorded on a child's record sheet.

A sticky note may be attached to a sample of the child's work such as their drawing or writing to help explain what they did and how.

A snapshot observation focuses on one aspect of the child's development.

A sticky note may be attached to a photo of the child achieving the particular skill to give more detail.

Figure 3.24: Sticky notes are a useful way to record information about a child

Time sample observations

Time sample observations are used to find out about how a child plays or about their behaviour. A brief observation of the child is written down on a prepared chart at regular intervals. Depending on what is being observed a note may be written every 5, 10 or 30 minutes. This method is used to show the frequency of specific behaviours.

For example, it might be used to observe a child where there is a concern about unwanted behaviour such as hitting other children. It could also be used to track who or what a child chooses to play with.

Table 3.13 shows the advantages and disadvantages of the time sample observation method.

Table 3.13: Advantages and disadvantages of a time sample observation

Advantages	Disadvantages
Can be used to show if the frequency of a child's particular behaviour changes over time.	May be difficult to remember to observe at each set time.
Can help to show what affects a child's behaviour.	Behaviour might not be seen if it happens outside of the set observation period.
Only takes a few moments to write what the child is doing at each interval.	Gives little detail of other aspects of development as observation has a specific focus.

Figure 3.25 shows an example of a time sample observation record.

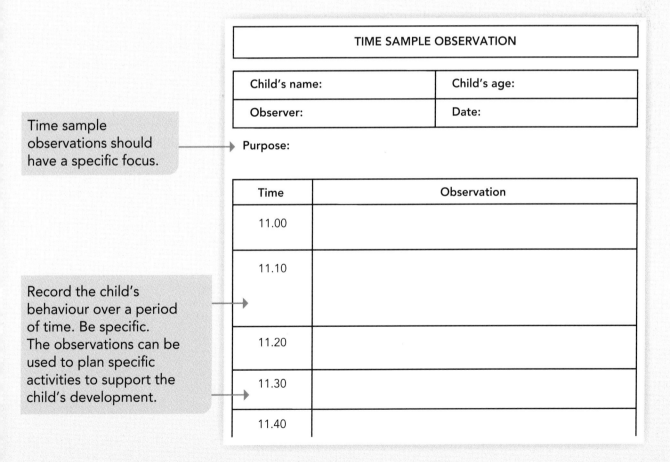

Time sample observations should have a specific focus.

Record the child's behaviour over a period of time. Be specific. The observations can be used to plan specific activities to support the child's development.

Figure 3.25: Example of a time sample observation record

Participative and non-participative observations

When carrying out an observation, the adult may be a **participative** or **non-participative** observer. A participative method means the adult is involved in the activity with the child. Non-participative means that the adult watches the child from a distance without the child being aware of them. You might participate or be watching from a distance when using any of the methods that have been discussed.

Table 3.14 shows the advantages and disadvantages of participative and non-participative observations.

Table 3.14: Advantages and disadvantages of participative and non-participative observations

	Advantages	Disadvantages
Participative	• The child will feel more comfortable with a familiar adult nearby. • Helpful in checklist observations as you can guide a child toward taking part in activity or using the skills you want to observe.	• It is difficult to write down everything that's happening using the narrative method at the same time as being involved with a child's play activity. • The child might act differently if they are aware they are being observed.
Non-participative	• Easier to record what you observe without any disruption, using any method of observation. • Children more likely to behave naturally.	• May not be able to hear what the child says. • Cannot influence what the child does or skills they use.

Stretch   1

Explain the strengths and limitations of being a non-participant when carrying out observations of children.

Methods of recording

Charts

A chart is made in advance of an observation. It is often based on a template. A chart is a closed method of observation because the observer has already decided what they will observe. Charts tend to be used for checklists or time samples. Checklists are often prepared with statements of development norms for a particular age group and area of development (see Figure 3.23). The observer places a tick against the relevant statement such as 'Can do up buttons'. Charts that are used for time sampling (see Figure 3.25) list the appropriate time intervals. There is a space for a comment against each time where the observer can write a note about what the child is doing.

As there is little space for writing on charts, you can use abbreviations if you are sure that others will understand them. For example, as the observer you might write 'Uses PG to draw circle' instead of 'Uses palmer grasp to draw a circle'. The notes do not need to be written in full sentences.

Written

Written methods of recording are used for narrative and snapshot observations. They are open methods because you do not know beforehand what you will observe. You should write down everything you see happening over a short period of time.

Narrative observations need to be detailed. They should be written as a running record, or commentary, as you watch a child. Always use the present tense, for example, 'Pria fills the jug' not 'Pria filled the jug'. In contrast, snapshot observations may be very brief at perhaps just one or two lines.

You do not always need to write in full sentences as long as the meaning is clear. As with charts, you can use abbreviations if you know that others will understand them as it is quicker to write using abbreviations. For example, 'Tom plays OD' (outdoors) or 'Masie sits in the BC' (book corner). It's important to practise writing quickly.

Child's work

It's not always easy to describe what a child has done or achieved. Using a sample of a child's work can add to what we know about a child. It could be a model, drawing or a recording of their music. Samples of work can be used as evidence on their own or attached to another method of observation as further evidence. For example, stating that a child draws detailed pictures doesn't make clear how detailed they are. Attaching their drawing to a written observation provides that additional evidence.

In Figure 3.26, Tia uses her finger to point as she counts each sweet. She counts to 6 correctly.

Figure 3.26: Example of how to use a photo as part of a snapshot observation

Photographs

Photos are frequently used in early years settings. They are useful as a digital snapshot of what a child can do but they don't tell the whole story. For example, a photo can't explain how a child approached an activity or record what they said. Photos are more helpful if they are attached to an observation with notes to explain them. Look at Figure 3.26. What would the photo tell you about this child's counting skills if there was no note attached?

Table 3.15 shows the rules you must follow when taking photos of children for observations.

Table 3.15: Rules for taking photos

Never	Always
• take a child's photograph without permission • use a personal phone or camera in a childcare setting.	• store photographs securely.

Over to you!　2

You have been asked to observe each of the following children:

- the gross motor skills of Liam aged two years
- the language skills of Priya aged three years
- the behaviour of Aadi aged four and a half years towards other children.

For each child:

a　Identify the observation method you would use and explain why that method is appropriate.

b　Explain how you would record each observation.

c　Explain whether a participative or non-participative method would be more appropriate for each observation.

Stretch　2

Explain the factors that you must consider when choosing the most appropriate method and ways to record the observation of a child.

Confidentiality

The most important thing to remember when observing children is that information about them must be kept confidential. **Confidentiality** is about:

- permission
- privacy of information. '

Parents or carers must give permission for their child to be observed. Usually, parents of children in early years settings will already have given permission for their children to be observed. This is because professionals carry out observations regularly.

If you plan to observe a child in person for your assessment (rather than one in a video provided by your teacher), it is still essential that you first seek permission to do so. Your observations should be anonymous (made private) by not using a child's full name or images of their face.

Privacy is about how the information recorded as part of the observation is stored and shared. Early years settings must store physical observation records securely in a locked cabinet in an office. Digital records must be stored in a password-protected file.

Sometimes observation records are shared, but information should only be with people who need to know about a child such as a parent, the manager of a childcare setting or a health professional. Parental permission is required before records can be shared.

Review your learning

Test your knowledge

1 Outline one or more possible reasons for observing children.

2 Explain the similarities and differences between the narrative method of observation and the snapshot method.

3 Explain why there could be confidentiality issues when carrying out snapshot observations.

4 Discuss the reasons for having sticky notes handy in an early years setting to note down observations.

5 Identify the most appropriate way to record the following methods of observation:

   a narrative

   b checklist

   c snapshot

   d time sample

6 Explain why it is important that other methods of observation are used alongside photos or a child's work.

What have you learnt?

	See section
• Observation and recording.	3.1

TA4

Plan and evaluate play activities for a child aged one to five years for a chosen area of development

Let's get started

Have you ever planned a play activity for a child? If so, was it at the correct level of difficulty for their age? Were the resources you used suitable? What else did you have to think about?

Figure 3.27: A play activity

What will you learn?

- Plan and evaluate play activities.

4.1 Plan and evaluate play activities

Plan play activities for a chosen area of development

Topic Area 4 gives you the opportunity to demonstrate (show) your activity planning skills for a child. You will put what you have learnt about children's development, types of play and methods of observation into action.

Chosen activity

The purpose of planning an activity is to help a child to progress in an area of their development. Your chosen play activity will depend upon what you discovered in your observation. Knowing about the child's stage of development, their age and what they like to do will help you to plan something suitable. If the activity is too simple, the child will soon get bored. If it's too hard, they will get frustrated because they can't complete the task or take part in the play. For example, it would not be appropriate to give a cutting out activity to a child who hasn't mastered the manipulative skills needed to use scissors.

Activity plans help you to organise your ideas. They are a statement of what you expect to achieve through the play activity (your aims) and how you would carry it out through an effective introduction, good timing and suitable resources.

Figure 3.28 shows an example of a planning form. You can use the headings in this template as a checklist for your own planning. You could design your own or one may be provided by your teacher. The planning template needs to have enough space for the detail of each part of your plan. Each of the headings will be explained in more detail in this section.

Let's get practical!   1

Design your own template for planning a play activity. You can use a sheet of paper or produce a digital template.

If you have already taken part in planning an activity for a child, use the information to practise filling in your template.

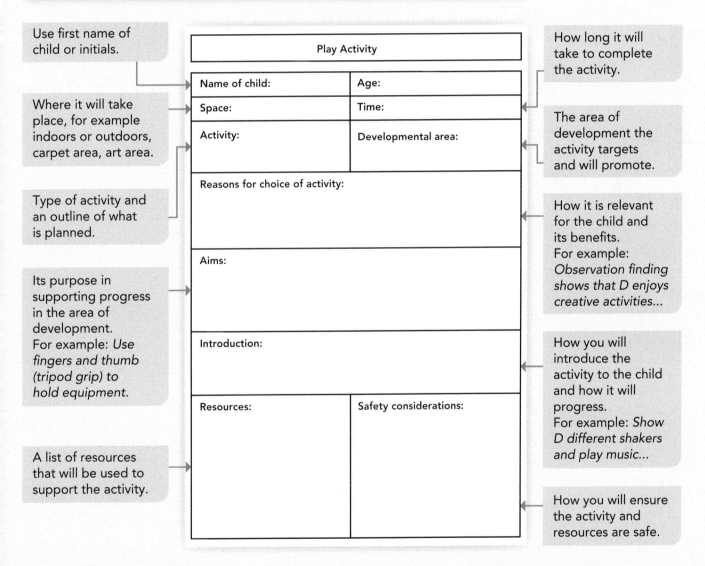

Use first name of child or initials.

Where it will take place, for example indoors or outdoors, carpet area, art area.

Type of activity and an outline of what is planned.

Its purpose in supporting progress in the area of development. For example: *Use fingers and thumb (tripod grip) to hold equipment.*

A list of resources that will be used to support the activity.

How long it will take to complete the activity.

The area of development the activity targets and will promote.

How it is relevant for the child and its benefits. For example: *Observation finding shows that D enjoys creative activities...*

How you will introduce the activity to the child and how it will progress. For example: *Show D different shakers and play music...*

How you will ensure the activity and resources are safe.

Play Activity

Name of child:	Age:
Space:	Time:
Activity:	Developmental area:

Reasons for choice of activity:

Aims:

Introduction:

| Resources: | Safety considerations: |

Figure 3.28: Example planning form

Reasons for choice

When choosing an activity, you need to consider how and where it could be carried out. You may have observed a child that you know in person, via a video link or by watching a video clip provided by your teacher.

To plan a suitable play activity, you must start with your observation of the child. Use these questions to help you choose a suitable activity. Ask yourself:

- What activities would be relevant to the area of development that's been identified as needing support in the observation? What activities would help them to progress?

- What are the norms of development for the child's age? What are the norms for the next stage of development? What activities will help them to progress? (For ideas for activities relevant to the three development areas see Topic Area 2, Section 2.2.)

- What activities are suitable for their age group?

- What does the child enjoy doing? What would be fun for them to do? What would capture their imagination?

Remember, that to be relevant and beneficial the play activity must help the child to practise and make progress in the area of development identified in your observation as needing support.

Figure 3.29 suggests some questions you could ask yourself to help you understand the benefits of the activity. Look back at Topic Area 2, Section 2.3 on how play benefits development.

You need to explain your reasons for choosing an activity. Look at Figure 3.28. In the box for 'Reasons for choice of activity', you can see that Daniel's key worker has explained how the planned activity links to the observation and how it will support the specific area of development in which Daniel needs help. The next stage of development for Daniel is to hold a crayon or glue stick using a pincer grasp rather than a palmer grasp so he will benefit from the practice.

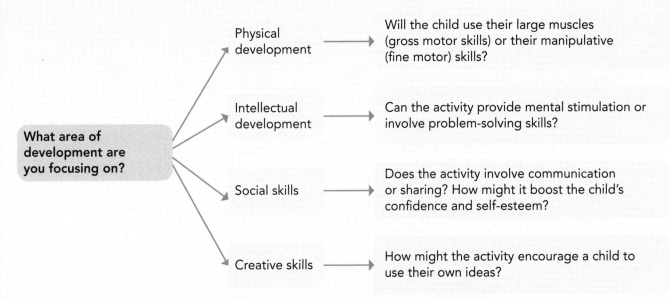

Figure 3.29: Decision tree: questions to understand the benefits of the activity

Over to you!   1

a   Outline activities that would support creative skills of children aged one to two years, three to four years and four to five years. The children are at their expected stage of development.

b   Explain three things you should consider when planning these activities.

c   Discuss how you could make sure that your activity is relevant to the development stage of the child.

Developmental area

The aims of your activity will relate to the area of development observed. Use the information you gathered from observing the child to compare their development with the expected developmental norms (see Topic Area 1). If your observation shows that the child has not met the expected development norms for their age, it may mean that they have a delay in that particular area of development. Some children may be advanced in their development. Remember that children vary and not all children reach a development norm at exactly the same age. Always take into consideration the stage of development the child has reached, not their age, so that you can support them toward their next development norms. Depending on what you observed you may need to use other reference books or the internet for further research.

Case study

Maira's first steps

Claire, a child minder, has observed the physical skills of Maira aged 16 months. Her narrative observation stated:

Maira pulls herself up by holding onto a chair. She stands for a few moments and then lets go. She stands for a few seconds but wobbles and looks unsteady. She takes three steps forwards towards her toy car. She stops, wobbles and falls down onto her bottom. Maira crawls the rest of the way over to the cupboard, pulls herself up, stretches her hand and picks up her car. She turns, stands still for a few seconds then drops down to her knees.

Figure 3.30: Maira and her ride-on toy

Claire decides to plan an activity where Maira will use a ride on toy that she must propel with her feet in and out of obstacles.

Check your understanding

1   What is the expected age norm for when children usually walk unaided?

2   Summarise Claire's findings from her observation of Maira.

3   How might the play activity benefit Maira's physical development?

Your observation will have given you some information about what the child likes to do. Does the child like to be active outdoors, or do they show an interest in playing with cars or dressing up? This can help you to decide on the type of activity that they would enjoy. There are lots of different activity ideas you could explore that can promote the same area of development.

Over to you! 2

Use the information in the photo and the attached observation to answer the questions.

a   Which area of Liam's development can you see in the photo?

b   Explain what this observation and photo tell you about Liam's development.

c   Explain ways to support Liam to progress in the featured area of development.

When L arrived at school he spent a few moments trying to undo his toggles. He almost cried when he couldn't manage them so was helped by Mrs T.

Figure 3.31: Liam, 4 years, trying to undo his toggles

Aims

Use your observation to help you to decide on the aim of your activity. First, look at your observation to help you identify what area of the child's development needs support. Then focus on the specific skill or aspect of development you wish to promote, and link it to the area of development. For example, your aim may be for a child to develop a new skill such as fastening and unfastening buttons.

Your aim should outline what the child will do and what you expect the outcome to be. It is very important that your aim is clear and specific because when you evaluate your activity plan you will need to measure how far your aim is likely to be met. For example, this aim is not specific and it would be difficult to measure whether the aim can be achieved:

'Zac will count in order and match numerals.'

A better, more specific aim would be:

'Zac will count from one to five in the correct order and match numerals to sets of objects one to five.'

Look back at Figure 3.28 to help you.

Timing

Whatever play activity you plan, it is important that you take into consideration the time it will take. It is helpful to break the activity into parts and think about time needed for each one:

- the introduction

- developing the activity

- for the child to help to put things away

- for the child to talk about what they have done.

Think about giving a child time to develop their ideas but also make sure that you vary the activity to keep their interest and prevent them getting bored. You need to think about the age of the child. A one-year-old child may only be able to concentrate for 2 to 3 minutes whilst for a four year old it could be around 8 to 12 minutes.

Safety considerations

You looked at types of childhood accidents and ways to minimise the risk to children in Unit R058. When planning an activity consider:

- the space where the activity will take place (indoor and outdoor)

- the equipment, materials and toys

- how you will supervise the activity.

Check the space where the activity will take place before it starts (see Table 3.16). Even as the activity develops, advice can be given on ways to remain alert to any changes in the space. There are particular risks outdoors because the area might be used by others.

Table 3.16: What to look for before and during the activity

Possible risks	
Indoors	**Outdoors**
• Slippery floors around water play or art areas • Clutter left on the floor • Loose flooring such as rugs • Objects on high shelving that could fall • The space is too small for the activity	• Gates left open or broken fences • Traffic entering an area • Animal faeces in garden areas or sand boxes • Hazards left around such as broken glass or debris • Plants that are toxic

Always check large equipment for safety. Outdoor climbing frames and play equipment must have a safe surface underneath in case children fall. Check wheeled toys to make sure there are no loose screws or sharp parts on them. Stepping stones or low balancing bars should be stable so they don't wobble whilst being used.

Small equipment and tools should be in good condition. Discard them if there are breaks or sharp edges that could hurt a child. Wooden construction blocks must be smooth with no splinters. Scissors or knives should have rounded ends.

Some materials can be harmful and if swallowed could make children very ill or may be fatal. Some can cause burns if they get on the skin or in eyes. For example, paints and glue are not always safe for children. Paints and glue must carry a non-toxic label to show they are safe to use.

Your choice of arts and craft materials will differ according to the age of the child. Small objects such as beads or buttons can cause choking in under threes. At that age children often put small objects in their mouths and could choke. They may even put them in ears or up noses. Play dough is a great activity for older children but not suitable for under twos who might want to eat it.

Toys used should carry a safety label such as the Lion Mark or the CE symbol. These show that the toy has been tested for safety. For more information on safety labelling see Unit R057, Topic Area 4, Section 4.3.

You must only include equipment or toys in your planning that are suitable for the age of the child. Toys have an age advice label which clearly shows if it is not suitable for children under three. Some toys have small parts or bits that could break off and be choking hazards. Soft toys may have fur that comes off and could be swallowed causing choking.

Supervision is crucial for safety. It means that the adult is keeping an eye on how the child is playing, using equipment and on making sure the area stays clean and safe. Your plan may require the adult to be closely involved in the activity or watching from a little distance, but they must remain constantly alert. Depending on your activity, your plans may show:

- how to make sure the child understands the rules before starting the activity – for example, not throwing sand or not walking around with scissors in their hand

Figure 3.32: Children playing in a sandpit

- that you know what the child is capable of – for example, providing a suitably sized trike

- how to check for safety as they play – for example, mopping up water that has spilled or removing trip hazards

- ways to show children how to use materials and equipment safely – for example, how to handle scissors, or use a knife or saw.

Let's get practical!   2

Use a computer to produce a poster that could be used in an early years setting as a reminder before carrying out a play activity. Include three safety checks to carry out in an indoor setting and three safety checks to carry out in an outdoor setting.

Appropriate resources

Resources means everything you need to carry out a play activity. That includes the space you choose, which should be appropriate for the planned activity.

Some play activities may require a specific type of space. Think about activities that may need:

- a natural outdoor environment where the child can be active, for example digging or exploring the natural world by finding mini beasts

- a messy play area for painting and gluing, or for using play dough or clay

- a large space where the child can be active to practise gross motor skills, for example by playing a ball game

- a comfortable floor area where a child can concentrate, such as a carpet space for sharing books, or responding to music or construction activities.

Once you have decided on your activity you need to think about the materials you would need. Many activities can be supported by recycled materials, pieces of fabric or discarded hats or clothing for dressing up. Play dough can be made rather than bought.

Some activities require specific equipment or tools. For example:

- water play: containers for filling, emptying and pouring

- art and craft: paint brushes and scissors

- physical play: large equipment such as climbing frames, balancing bikes, trikes or stepping stones; small equipment may include hoops, beanbags or balls.

You might plan to use resources such as puzzles, tabletop games, musical instruments or soft play toys (for example, soft balls, teddies or puppets).

It's a good idea to test out resources to check if they would be suitable for the activity. Children will get frustrated if the resources don't work well. For example:

- Is the resource suitable for the activity? A glue stick would be unsuitable for making a cardboard model; some types of paint do not work on plastic.

- Are the tools the correct size for the child? Do they work? Scissors should cut well; a toy plastic hammer or screwdriver won't work if a child is making a wooden model.

- Are the toys age appropriate? Small construction bricks will be too fiddly for children under three years of age and larger blocks would not challenge children aged four to five years.

How the activity will be introduced to the child

How you introduce the activity is really important. It should capture the child's interest so that they are excited and keen to get involved. There are many ways to do this so it's important to spend some time thinking of the best way. For example, you could plan to start by telling a story, reciting a rhyme or using a storyboard (see Figure 3.33). For a painting or modelling activity you might spark a child's interest by showing resources and materials that they can't wait to get their hands on.

Figure 3.33: What kind of activity could be introduced through storytelling?

The way you introduce the activity will influence your own involvement in the activity. For example, you could plan to:

- provide set out resources and step back to allow the child to lead their own play

- lead the play by demonstration, such as rolling a ball down a tube then encouraging a child to do the same

- play alongside, such as cooking with a child or planting seeds with them.

Whichever method you plan it is important that you support the child to make their own decisions about their play as it develops. You could include ways to guide the activity such as suggesting resources that could be added to help the play along. Questions also are a good way to do this. Your planning might include questions that could be asked such as 'Which colour do you think would look best?' or 'What could you use to make the wheels?'.

Stretch   **1**

Plan ways to introduce each of the following activities, giving your reasons.

1. Dev is planning to plant cress seeds with a child aged three years to promote their thinking skills.

2. Saanvi is planning to organise an obstacle course for a child aged four years to encourage climbing, jumping and balancing skills.

3. Amy is planning a hand printing activity with a child aged two years to promote their creative skills.

Capturing feedback/recording of the activity

How to evaluate plans for play activities

Evaluation is a way to measure the likely success of your planning. It is a process where you invite the views of others and use your own thoughts to make a judgement about how effective the activity might be in achieving your aims. You must consider the strengths and weaknesses of each aspect of your planning and suggest where you could make improvements.

Using feedback from others

Feedback can be helpful from different people who have an interest and knowledge of child development. For example, you might present your plans to the parents or carers of a child you have planned the activity for or to an early years professional. You could discuss your plans with them or ask for written feedback to gather their views. They will be able to identify which aspects of your planning are likely to support the child well and may suggest aspects that could be improved. Another useful method might be to prepare questions for them to answer about each aspect of your plan.

Feedback from peers is also a helpful source of information. You could share plans with a friend or even present your planning to your class and invite their feedback. Whichever method you choose, it is important to keep notes that can contribute to your evaluation.

Using self-reflection

Self-reflection means observing your own skills and abilities to come to a conclusion about the strengths of your plan and anything you feel less confident about. The process helps you to improve skills and is an essential part of the role of an early years professional. When you reflect on your planning think about each aspect in turn, for example 'Will the activity support the area of development identified?' or 'Will there be enough time to carry it out?'. As you reflect on each aspect of your plan, you will be able to identify those you are confident about and are likely to be successful, and those you could improve upon.

Were the aims met?

Your aims are what you plan to do and how you planned to achieve them. Revisit the paragraph 'Aims' that discusses how to identify your aims. Once you have gathered feedback from others and completed your self-reflection, you can make a judgement about how successful you were in achieving your aims. You need to consider ways that your planned activity will be effective in supporting the child to improve in the area of development you have targeted. Give reasons why you chose a particular activity, exploring how the activity could benefit the child. For example, you may have observed the child starting to use simple sentences so have planned an activity using puppets. You should explain ways that the activity will encourage verbal communication. Also refer to other aspects of your plans such as how you will introduce the activity and the resources you plan to use, explaining how they help the child to take part in the activity and practise and improve their skills and abilities.

Successes and strengths/weaknesses

You must come to a conclusion about parts of your planning that are likely to go well and things that may not work quite so well. It is important that you recognise your strengths but also recognise where you could make improvements. Here are some things you could ask yourself as you consider the feedback from others and your own reflections:

- How effective is the introduction?
- Will the space be suitable?
- Is the timing appropriate?
- How will the resources contribute to the success of the activity?
- Will the activity be safe?

Changes or recommendations to improve activity and planning

You must show what you have learnt by planning the activity. It is likely that there will be some aspects of the activity that may not work as well as you expect. Understanding the strengths and weaknesses of your activity will help you to suggest possible changes (make recommendations) to improve it. This is good practice because it helps you to develop your skills. For example, you might consider a different way to introduce your activity or change the resources you would use. If you felt the activity might not promote the targeted area of development, you could even suggest an alternative activity. Remember that however well you plan, there are likely to be aspects of your activity that could be improved upon.

Stretch   2

Explain the cycle of observation, planning, and the delivering of play activities and their purpose in supporting children's development.

Review your learning

Test your knowledge

1 Explain possible risks to children when playing:

   a indoors

   b outdoors.

2 Explain the importance of age-appropriate materials and toys.

3 Discuss two ways to seek feedback about your planned activity from others.

4 Explain why it's important to evaluate an activity.

5 Evaluate the importance of making recommendations to improve an activity.

What have you learnt?

	See section
• Plan and evaluate play activities.	4.1

Glossary

Accessibility: Able to be used by people with special educational needs or disabilities.

The preschool considered accessibility when choosing a new sand box; they chose a design that would allow a child using a wheelchair to be able to take part.

Accident: An unexpected event that causes injury or damage.

Mia was hurt in an accident yesterday – she fell down the stairs.

Activity plan: A statement of what you expect to achieve through the play activity (your aims) and how you plan to carry it out through an effective introduction, good timing and suitable resources.

Amniotic fluid: A yellow fluid (liquid) formed in the 12 days after conception to surround and protect the embryo and later the foetus.

The embryo is surrounded by amniotic fluid for protection.

Anaesthetic: A pain relief method, often in the form of medication.

An epidural is a popular anaesthetic in labour.

Anomaly: Something which is unusual or different from normal.

The couple went for the anomaly scan at 20 weeks.

Antenatal care: The medical care which is given to a woman during pregnancy.

After confirming her pregnancy, the doctor referred Amara to the antenatal clinic.

Antenatal clinic: Where pregnancy appointments take place.

Assisted birth/instrumental delivery: When forceps or a ventouse suction cup are used during birth to help with delivery.

The midwife told Diane about what would happen in an assisted birth.

Associate/associative play: Children talk together and use the same resources.

Associate play is the stage of play when children may share resources and talk but do not plan the play together.

Bacteria: Microorganisms that can cause diseases.

The children were asked to wash their hands to remove any bacteria.

Balance: The ability to control body movement.

AJ holds out his arms to help him balance as he walks across the log.

Balanced diet: Eating a variety of foods so your body takes in all the nutrients needed for healthy growth and development.

Saleh eats a balanced diet with lots of fruit and vegetables.

Barrier method of contraception: Barrier methods of contraception provide a physical obstruction that prevents sperm from reaching the egg.

Birth plan: A written record of a pregnant woman's preferred options during labour.

Michael and Samira sat down to work out their preferred birth plan.

Body language: Body movements, posture and facial expressions that show how a person is feeling.

Anya leaned forward, showing through her body language that she was listening.

Body Mass Index (BMI): A measure to work out whether or not an adult's weight is healthy by dividing their weight by their height. A healthy BMI is between 18.5 and 24.9.

Jess was told that it was likely her BMI was too high to conceive successfully.

Bottle feed: When a baby is fed with milk from a bottle.

Dads often enjoy bottle-feeding their babies.

Breastfeed: When a mother feeds her baby with milk from her breasts.

Breastfeeding is encouraged in the first few weeks of a baby's life.

Caesarean section: An operation to deliver a baby through a cut in the abdomen.

Sam had to have a caesarean section to deliver her twins.

Centile chart: A graph that shows a baby's expected pattern of growth.

The health visitor explained that their baby was in the lower range on the centile chart.

Cervix: The lower part of the uterus which leads to the vagina.

Checklist (tick list) observation: A list of development norms that the observer can check off as they observe the child's skills.

Circumference: The size of a baby's head (measured around the broadest part of the baby's forehead, above the ears and around the back of the head).

The health visitor measured the circumference of the baby's head.

Clinical examination: A medical examination to identify or diagnose a possible condition or disease.

The doctor carried out a clinical examination.

Club foot (talipes): When a baby's foot or feet turn inwards.

Hugh was born with talipes.

Conception: The point of fertilisation when an embryo starts to form and pregnancy begins.

Confidentiality: Keeping a person's private information secret.

Devi observed confidentiality by keeping information about the child in a locked cabinet.

Contagious: Of a disease that spreads from person to person.

Flu is a contagious illness.

Contraception: Using various methods to prevent pregnancy when having sex.

Contraction: A tightening of the muscles of the uterus.

She was having strong, regular contractions.

Cooperative play: Children play the same game or activity together.

The children discussed their play plans and worked towards the same goal in their cooperative play.

Coordination: The ability to move different parts of the body to carry out a movement or task.

Creative play: A way of expressing ideas and emotions through a play activity.

Dhanya designed and made a model in her creative play activity.

Diagnostic test: A test which is used to discover what is wrong and whether a baby has a specific condition.

The diagnostic test showed that their baby had a high chance of having a health condition.

Down's syndrome: A lifelong condition which causes a learning disability that can be mild to severe. It affects around 1 in 600 babies.

Durable: Can last for a long time and be used a lot without breaking or getting damaged.

The childminder chose a new sand box that was made of durable plastic, as the old one had cracked.

Embryo: The fertilised egg developing in its mother's womb up to the first eight weeks of pregnancy.

Epidural: A form of pain relief during labour which is given by an anaesthetist.

I wrote in my birth plan that I would like to have an epidural.

Episiotomy: A cut which is made in the area between the vagina and anus to help with childbirth. This is stitched after the birth.

The doctor gave her an episiotomy to help with the delivery of her baby.

Fallopian tube: Either one of the pair of tubes in a woman's body that carry the egg to the uterus.

Fertilisation: When the woman's egg joins with the man's sperm; this process happens in the fallopian tubes.

Artificial fertilisation is an option if a couple can't conceive naturally.

Fertility (fertile): The ability to conceive and produce babies.

Lots of different factors can affect men's and women's fertility.

Fine motor skills: Use and coordination of the small muscles in the body.

Ajay used fine motor skills to control the pencil to draw a circle.

Fitness: Being healthy and physically strong.

Jenna demonstrated her fitness when she climbed to the top of the frame.

Foetus: An unborn baby more than eight weeks after fertilisation, after the organs have started to develop.

Follicle: The part of the ovary in which an egg grows and develops.

Fontanelles: The soft areas on a baby's head where the skull bones have not yet fused together. One is at the front of the head at the top, and the other towards the back. These soft areas allow the skull some flexibility during childbirth. The skull bones gradually fuse together in the first year or so.

You must be very gentle when you wash a baby's head as the fontanelles are so soft.

Food poisoning: Illness caused by eating bacteria in contaminated food.

Jamie always washes his hands before preparing meals to help to prevent food poisoning.

Forceps: A metal instrument similar to a pair of tongs which are made in the shape of a baby's head to help with delivery.

The doctor used forceps to deliver the baby.

Gestational diabetes: A condition in which a woman has too much glucose (sugar) in her blood during pregnancy. This can cause a range of issues such as jaundice, pre-eclampsia or premature birth.

Kerry and her unborn baby were monitored very closely because she had gestational diabetes.

GP (General Practitioner): A doctor who is based at a local surgery.

Riz went to see her GP to confirm her pregnancy.

Gross motor skills: Use and coordination of the large muscles in the body.

Climbing the tree involved using gross motor skills.

Hand–eye coordination: Using the eyes to coordinate the movements of the hands.

Maya used hand–eye coordination when she slotted in the puzzle piece.

Harm: Injury or damage.

Button batteries can cause serious harm if swallowed.

Hazard: Something that may cause you or others harm.

Uncovered ponds are a hazard.

Heart murmur: Sounds made by blood swishing in or near the heart.

The couple were told that their baby might have a heart murmur.

Holistic: Concerning the development of the whole child: physical, intellectual and social.

The nursery said that they monitored the holistic development of each child.

Hormones: There are various types of hormones; they are chemicals which are produced by the body to help influence how cells and tissues work.

Identical twins: Two children born to the same mother at the same time who developed from the same egg.

Jayden and Robbie are identical twins – nobody can tell them apart.

Imaginative play: Play involving being creative and inventive.

The children took part in an imaginative play, pretending to be animals.

Immune system: The body's defence system against disease and infection.

Gaurik has a strong immune system; he rarely gets ill.

Immunisation/vaccination: A way of protecting a person from a disease by giving them an injection of a vaccine.

Zofia had not had all her immunisations before she became pregnant.

Implantation: When a fertilised egg burrows into the lining of the uterus.

Implantation day may vary depending on when you ovulated and when you had sex.

Impotence: A medical condition when a man can't have or can't maintain an erection and so can't have sex.

Infant: A baby aged 0–12 months.

Cow's milk should not be given to infants as it is not suitable for babies until they are one year of age.

Intellectual development: How children think, solve problems and respond to information.

Intrauterine: Inside the uterus.

An IUD is an example of an intrauterine contraceptive method.

IVF (in vitro fertilisation): An artificial way of having support to help couples to conceive a baby.

As they were unable to conceive after two years of trying, the couple decided to ask the GP whether they were eligible for IVF.

Labour: The process of having a baby from the start of contractions to the delivery of the placenta.

Mel was in labour for 12 hours with her first baby, but this was much shorter second time around.

Lactose: The sugar in cow's milk.

Agnes is lactose intolerant so she can't drink cow's milk.

Lanugo: A type of soft, fine hair covering that develops on the baby's body at around the 22nd week of pregnancy.

Lifestyle choices: Choices about how a person decides to behave, for example smoking or taking drugs.

Fin regretted some of the lifestyle choices he had made in his 20s, as they may have affected his fertility.

Listeriosis: A bacterial infection caused by listeria, a bacterium found in fermented cheese.

A woman may become ill with listeriosis after eating contaminated food.

Manipulative play: Play that involves the use of hands and fingers.

The children improved their fine motor skills through manipulative play.

Menstrual cycle: The monthly process of ovulation and menstruation in a woman's body.

To try to work out when she was most fertile, Josie and her partner decided to track her menstrual cycle.

Menstruation: Period (the monthly blood flow from a woman's uterus when a woman is not pregnant).

Menstruation usually takes place once a month.

Milestone: The stage of development that most children reach at a certain age.

Toby has reached the expected milestone for his age.

Miscarriage: The loss of a pregnancy before 24 weeks.

Aliza suffered a miscarriage during her last pregnancy.

Narrative observation: A detailed written description of what is being observed over a short period of time.

Neural tube: Part of the central nervous system, formed in the embryo shortly after conception.

Non-identical twins: Two children born to the same mother at the same time who developed from two different eggs.

Lucy and Tom are non-identical twins, as twins of a different sex cannot be identical.

Non-participative: To be apart from the action.

He stood back from the play as a non-participative observer.

Norm: The usual pattern of development that children follow.

Lena met her expected development norm when she started to walk at 14 months.

Notifiable disease: A disease that must be reported to a government authority.

Mumps is a notifiable disease.

Nourish: To provide with the food and nutrients necessary for growth.

The foetus is nourished by the placenta whilst it is growing.

Nutrients: The nourishment we get from food that is needed for healthy growth and development.

Formula milk provides all the nutrients a baby needs to grow and develop.

Obese: Having a body mass index (BMI) of 30 or over.

The doctor told Alex that he needs to lose weight because he is obese.

Obesity: Being very overweight with too much body fat.

The Government was concerned about rising obesity in the population.

Objective: Information that is not influenced by personal opinions or views.

Recording what you see without giving your opinion leads to an objective observation.

Observation: A record of what has been seen.

Tracey carried out an observation of Dev as he played in the sand.

Oestrogen: A female reproductive hormone.

Ovary: Either one of the pair of organs in a woman's body that produces eggs.

Ovulate: To produce an egg from an ovary.

Sasha was using a calendar to calculate when she would ovulate.

Ovulation: The point in a woman's menstrual cycle when an egg is released.

Palmer grasp: When a child holds an object such as a crayon in their palm with their thumb and fingers wrapped around it.

Nimra held the brush in a palmer grasp to brush her hair.

Parallel play: The stage of play when children play alongside but not with each other.

Tom and Josef, aged two, sit side by side building their own models in parallel play.

Participative: To take part in the action.

She joined in the children's activity as a participative observer.

Penis: The part of a man's body that is used for urinating and sex.

Phonics: A method of teaching children to read by learning the sounds represented by letters.

Physical play: Play involving the coordination and movement of the muscles in the body.

Physical play helps children to be fit and active.

Physiological: A normal characteristic of a living thing.

Maddie was told that being emotional was a normal physiological part of pregnancy.

Pincer grasp: Picking up a small object using the first finger and thumb.

Micah used a pincer grasp to pick up the small stone.

Placenta: An organ which develops inside the uterus during pregnancy, providing oxygen and nutrients to the foetus through the umbilical cord.

Placenta praevia: When the placenta is low in the uterus and blocks the entrance to the cervix.

Play activity: A planned task for an individual child that supports the development of their skills and abilities.

Postnatal care: The care given to a new mother and her baby after birth.

Amayah told her sister that she had had excellent postnatal care after the baby was born.

Pre-conception: Before fertilisation.

Women are advised to take folic acid pre-conception as this is important for the health of the baby.

Pre-conception health: The health influences and risk factors of both parents who are planning to conceive, for example type of diet or drinking alcohol.

For her pre-conception health, Gemma was advised to give up smoking before trying to conceive.

Pre-eclampsia: A potentially serious condition which is caused by problems with the placenta leading to a loss of nutrients for the baby.

The blood test revealed that Jenny was at risk of pre-eclampsia.

Premature baby: A baby born before it should be.

Nic and Bayram had a premature baby that had to spend some time in the baby care unit.

Progesterone: A female reproductive hormone.

Reproduction: The process of having babies.

The biology teacher announced that today we would be learning about human reproduction.

Risk: The possibility of harm being caused.

Amira cut the children's grapes into quarters to help to prevent the risk of choking.

Risk assessment: A list of potential hazards and the measures in place to help prevent accidents and harm.

The childminder made a risk assessment of the garden.

Salmonella: A type of bacteria.

Charlotte got salmonella poisoning from drinking a smoothie that had a raw egg in it.

Saturated fat: Fats that come from animals.

Screening: A way of identifying people who may have an increased chance of having a condition or disease.

Gina was sent for screening as her pregnancy had a risk of some health conditions.

Screening test: A test that checks an unborn baby's development and identifies the risk of specific health problems or conditions.

All mothers are offered screening tests during their pregnancy.

Self-esteem: An individual's confidence in their own abilities and worth.

Grace's self-esteem was boosted when she first rode her bike without help.

Self-image: A person's sense of who they are.

Antoni is a confident child with positive self-image.

Self-reflection: Observing your own skills and abilities to come to a conclusion about the strengths and weaknesses of your plan.

Seminal vesicle: One of a pair of glands which are situated each side of the bladder in a man's body. During ejaculation, the seminal vesicles add fluid and nutrients to the sperm to produce semen.

Show: A sign that labour has started, when the plug of mucus in the cervix is released.

Pola called her birth partner to say that she'd had a show.

SIDS (sudden infant death syndrome): When an apparently healthy baby dies without a clear medical explanation in the first six months of their life.

Controlling the temperature of the baby's bedroom is one of the ways of preventing SIDS.

Sign: Evidence that something is happening.

Snapshot observation: When a brief note is made about a child to capture something they do or a skill they use.

Social development: How children develop their communication skills, and form relationships and friendships.

Socialisation: Learning social skills, like good manners or family customs.

Children learn socialisation when surrounded by others.

Solids: Mashed-up or pureed food introduced to babies.

Solitary play: The stage of play when a young child plays alone and does not join in play with other children.

One-year-old Carrie ignores others around her as she concentrates on her toys in solitary play.

Sperm duct/epididymis: A long tube in a man's body in which the sperm matures and is stored.

Sterilise: The process of killing harmful bacteria, for example on babies' bottles.

Before making up the bottles with babies' milk, it is important to sterilise them.

Stillbirth: A birth when the baby is born dead after a pregnancy of 24 weeks or more.

Subjective: Information based on personal opinions and views.

The observation was subjective because it expressed the observer's own view of the child.

Symptom: A feeling of illness, or a physical or mental change, that is caused by something.

Desi had all of the symptoms of chickenpox around ten days after his first visit to nursery.

Testes (singular testis)/testicle: The part of a man's body that produces and stores sperm.

Testosterone: A male hormone which helps with sperm production.

Time sample observation: When information is captured about what a child is doing at particular times of the day.

Toxoplasmosis: A parasitic disease caused by eating infected food.

You should always wash your fruit and vegetables before eating to prevent toxoplasmosis.

Trimester: Any of the three-month periods that a pregnancy is divided into.

The second trimester is usually the easiest.

Type 2 diabetes: A condition in which the level of sugar in the blood becomes too high and the body is unable to produce enough of the hormone insulin to lower it. This means that a person's blood sugar level keeps rising and they need to inject insulin to bring it down.

The GP told him that he had developed Type 2 diabetes, but that he may be able to reverse this if he changed his diet.

Umbilical cord: A long structure, a bit like a tube, that connects an unborn baby to its mother's placenta.

The umbilical cord was clamped and cut after the baby was born and the placenta delivered.

Unsaturated fat: Fats that usually come from plants or fish.

Urethra: The tube that carries urine from the bladder out of the body. In men it also carries sperm.

Uterus/womb: The part of a woman's body in which a baby develops before it is born.

Vaccine: Something injected into a person's body to protect them against a disease.

The girls are having their rubella vaccine at school tomorrow.

Vagina: The passage in a woman's body that connects the outer sex organs to the uterus.

Value for money: Something that is worth the amount it costs to buy it.

The trainer cups that the nursery bought were good value for money.

Vas deferens: The tube that sperm pass through on their way out of a man's body.

Ventouse: A type of suction cup, which attaches to a baby's head, used to help to deliver a baby.

Rick told his mum that their baby had needed a ventouse delivery.

Vernix: A white waxy protective substance which covers the baby's skin while it is in the uterus.

Waters break: A sign that labour has started, when the amniotic fluid is released from the amniotic sac.

Jessica's waters broke when she was in the supermarket.

Wean: Start to move babies from milk towards solid food.

Jeanette decided to wean her baby after talking to the health visitor.

Index